Teach
More -
Faster!

MADELINE HUNTER

University of California, Los Angeles

CORWIN PRESS, INC.
A Sage Publications Company
Thousand Oaks, California

Other publications by the same author:

Mastery Teaching
Motivation Theory for Teachers
Retention Theory for Teachers
Discipline That Develops Self-Discipline
Teach for Transfer
Aide-ing in Education
Improved Instruction
Improving Your Child's Behavior
Parent-Teacher Conferencing
Mastering Coaching and Supervision

Teach More - Faster!
© Copyright 1967 by Madeline Hunter

Printed in the United States of America.
Thirty-Fifth Printing, September 1996

Hunter, Madeline C.
    Teach more — faster! / Madeline Hunter.
        p.   cm.
    Originally published : El Segundo, Calif. : TIP Publications, c 1967.
    ISBN 0-8039-6318-1   (pbk. : alk. paper)
    1. Learning, Psychology of .   2. Teaching.   I. Title.
LB1060.H86   1995
370.15'23 — dc20   95-6573

For information on the complete Madeline Hunter Collection, please contact:

CORWIN PRESS, INC.
A Sage Publications Company
2455 Teller Road
Thousand Oaks, CA 91320-2218
Call: 805-499-9774 Fax: 805-499-0871

FOREWORD

Psychological knowledge that will result in significantly increased learning of students is now available for teachers. In most cases, this knowledge remains unused because it is written in language that takes an advanced statistician to decode, or is buried in research journals in university libraries.

This book is one of a series written to make this important knowledge available to the classroom teacher. As such, it makes no attempt to achieve comprehensive coverage of the subject, but endeavors to interpret that knowledge which is most useful in the daily decisions of teachers. The purist in learning theory may complain that some generalization are over-simplified. Our answer would be that understanding a theory in simple form is necessary to the desire to search for increasing ramifications and complexities. The reader must also be warned that decisions based on learning theory are decisions of HOW to teach. These decisions can be made only AFTER the teacher has made decisions of WHAT content to teach and WHICH objectives are appropriate for the learner in that content area.

In other words, once a teacher has identified an appropriate educational destination for the learner, knowledge of learning theory will reveal the most effective, efficient, and economical route to reach that destination.

Appreciation is expressed to Miss Margaret Brown and Mr. Doug Russell for their insightful suggestions, to Mrs. Margaret Devers for her ability to translate rough copy into finished manuscript, and to all the University Elementary teachers who have insisted, "help me understand that!"

Madeline Hunter

To the University Elementary School Staff who have
taught me,
fought me,
supported me,
stimulated me,
encouraged me,
this book is fondly dedicated.

TEACH MORE —
FASTER!

There ought to be some way to make this job of teaching easier and more predictably successful. There is!

Of all the factors important in learning, by far the most important is *your ability* as a teacher to *promote* that learning in your students. The profession of teaching, in fact, is based upon the application of knowledge from psychology, from curriculum theory, and from the academic disciplines as it becomes fused in the teaching-learning act. The difference between teaching and keeping school or supervising students while they learn lies primarily in the use of funded knowledge to make learning or achievement of an educational goal, easier, more rapid, and more predictably successful for a student. It is the difference between just arranging for a person to have access to a pool in the hope he will learn to swim or giving him expert instruction to see that he does.

Teaching is a learned profession not a genetically based or "God given" trait. Of course individuals vary in aptitudes and interests which make it harder or easier to become competent in the profession of teaching, but teachers are *not* born, they're *made*. This book was written to have a part in the making. After reading it, you should:

1. Possess information about the psychology of learning which is relevant to your daily teaching.
2. Understand what you read so it is meaningful to your classroom performance.
3. Be able to apply your knowledge to an infinite number of learning situations.
4. Analyze your daily classroom problems to see where this book can provide help.
5. Use this information plus what you already know from experience, and, in terms of your own teaching style, develop some productive courses of action.
6. Make a judgment as to which course of action is best for you and your students at any given moment in time and *act*; then evaluate the success of your action and make any necessary modifications.

1

In short you should find teaching easier and more predictably successful.

Your achievement of all these goals would be measureable if we could observe your performance in number six. Obviously it is impossible to follow you into your classroom to see how successful this book was. You will, however, be able to evaluate your performance in the first three goals by means of the classroom situations described in this book, and your selection of answers to questions concerning them. We will depend on you to take it from there to reality. Should you want to compare what you now know with what you have learned from reading this book, turn to the test on page 75 and check your current state of knowledge before you start.

All set? Let's begin!

The problems of any learning task arise from two sources: 1) the material to be learned, 2) the student who is to accomplish that learning. For purposes of inspection and analysis we must separate these two factors so we, as teachers, can learn how to deal with each. It is essential, however, to remember that in real life they are never separated. Learning does not occur without interaction between the student and the task, each having an effect on the other. To be successful the teacher must take both into account. At times the teacher may need to focus more sharply on important knowledge about the particular student which can be used to assist his learning. An example of this would be the fact that the student is very tired, he hates math, or he learns best when he can use concrete material.

At other times, teaching decisions may be more intensely focused on the actual material in the learning assignment. An example of this would be the order in which the material is best presented, the relationship (or lack of it) of this material to other material which already has been learned, or the length and complexity of the material. Again we need to stress the constant interaction between student and task; this is the process of learning. One never exists without the other; we separate them only for the purpose of our own learning just as we separate study of the circulatory system from study of the digestive system knowing that each has an effect on the other and that they always function together in the human body.

Other books in this series of Theory into Practice have been concerned with the learner and the factors in his environment which the teacher can arrange to increase his learning. Rather than focusing primarily on the learner, this book will begin by focusing on the material to be learned and identify the properties of that material which can propel or interfere with successful accomplishment of the learning task.

To increase your speed of learning we will present some important information about learning tasks, then ask a question to see how well we have communicated with you. You will select an answer to the question and turn to the page indicated which will tell you if your answer is correct and why. Let's try it.

In this book we are going to focus on the learning task, because:

a. The learning task is the most important aspect of teaching. . . . Turn to page 4, top

b. The learning task can be the same, but students are different. . Turn to page 4, bottom

c. To be a successful teacher we should know the properties of learning tasks which are related to increasing or interfering with learning . . . . Turn to page 5, top

d. What you teach (content) is more important than how you teach (methodology) . . . . Turn to page 5, bottom

a. You said the learning task is the most important aspect of teaching.

It's one of the two most important aspects, that's for sure! The other important aspect is the student who has to accomplish the task. One aspect may seem more important at some times especially if you as a teacher are having a problem "getting it across," but neither one is always the more important. Turn back to the question on page 3, and select an answer that will justify your reading this book.

b. You said the learning task remains the same but students are different.

The fact that you know students learn differently puts you ahead of most of the people in the world. This "differentness" has a direct relationship to the learning task. Learning to pilot a new kind of plane is quite a different learning task for an airline pilot and for someone who has never been in a plane. As a result, the teacher must focus on the learner *and* on the task. Turn back to the question on page 3, and select an answer that will explain why you are taking the time to read a book that is devoted primarily to the properties of the task which is to be learned.

c. **You said to be a successful teacher we must know the properties of learning tasks which are related to increasing or interfering with learning.**

RIGHT YOU ARE! (Positive reinforcement, we want you to continue to choose the correct answer. If you don't know what we mean by positive reinforcement you should read *Reinforcement Theory for Teachers*, which is an important book in this series.) A successful teacher must inspect each learning task or assignment to identify the properties that can be utilized to make the job easier for the learner so his success is more probable and his learning is more rapid. The teacher must also be aware of the properties of the task that could interfere with successful accomplishment so these factors can be minimized or eliminated. You have demonstrated you learn well from reading so you are ready to begin reading about the properties of learning tasks that can be used to increase success in your classroom. Turn to page 6.

d. **You said what you teach (content) is more important than how you teach (methodology).**

A lot of people would agree with you. Others maintain that how you teach is more important. To argue that it is more important for a teacher to know mathematics than to know how to teach it is, we think, like arguing that your right leg is more important than your left leg when you run. Unless you have both you're not going to run anywhere and unless you know both content and methodology you're not very likely to be a successful teacher. Turn back to the question on page 3, and select an answer that will show you believe in strengthening each one of your teaching "legs."

Motivation

Obviously, a students motivation (intent or desire to learn) is one of the most important factors that influences how much and how rapidly he learns. This factor is so important a full book in this series, *Motivation Theory for Teachers*, has been devoted to the six factors which a teacher can adjust in the classroom so a students motivation to learn will be increased. It is important to remember that if motivation doesn't exist, learning probably won't either. If on the other hand motivation becomes excessive (or obsessive), anxiety can be generated that will interfere with learning. If your job depended on your answering all of our questions correctly, you would be highly motivated to learn, but you would be so anxious about making a mistake your feelings would interfere with your learning.

By reading the book *Motivation Theory for Teachers* every teacher can become aware of the factors in her classroom which can be used to increase students motivation to learn. By manipulating these factors you can "inspire" instead of "perspire" in the teaching role, which will make the difference between a "headstart" or "handicap" as you apply what you learn in this book.

There has been a great deal of criticism of universities where professors talk about teaching but are poor teachers themselves. The same criticism could be directed to a book that was concerned with how to increase learning but didn't practice what it preached. (We remember our psychology professor who lectured more than an hour on the theme that the average attention span is about 20 minutes.) Consequently, to avoid "talking about" rather than "doing" we are going to give you a learning task. From your first hand experience in this task you will discover properties of assignments that will aid or hinder learning. We will help you identify those properties, teach you their psychologically correct names, show you how they exist in many learning tasks, and help you know some ways to use these properties to make the teaching-learning act in your own classroom more predictably successful.

You need to have a pencil or a pen available so take time now to get one. Your assignment will be to learn a list of words. You will read them at your regular reading speed, then turn the page and write the words you remember (have learned) on the lines provided. Be sure you do exactly as you are directed or typical learning patterns will not emerge and you will not discover for yourself the important properties of a learning task that can propel or impede learning. Not following directions on the learning task we set will make your real learning job in this book more difficult for you.

Remember your task is to read the list of words *once* at your regular reading speed and then on the following page write as many of the words as you can remember. Try to put each word on the line which represents the place the word occupies on the list, i.e., the first word on the first line, the second word on the second line and the last word on the last line. Ready? Turn to the next page.

Read the words *once*

kef

lak

mil

nir

vek

lun

nem

beb

sar

fif

Turn to the next page and write them.

Write the words you just read:

1. _____

2. _____

3. _____

4. _____

5. _____

6. _____

7. _____

8. _____

9. _____

10. _____

Don't look back yet but turn to the next page.

You didn't expect the list to be nonsense syllables did you? If you're like most of us you didn't do very well on that list. You probably got the first and second one correct, mixed up the third and fourth, broke down completely after the fifth and (if you were lucky) remembered the last one. Do you want to look back and see how you did? It's all right now, go ahead. You don't need to, however, unless you want to.

You are already beginning to formulate some ideas of what makes a learning task difficult aren't you? We will check these out with you in just a few minutes.

Now let's turn to your next learning task which is another list of words. The directions are the same. Read them through once at your regular reading speed, turn the page and write them down as you remember them. Ready? Turn the page.

Read these words once.

cat

fan

sit

run

pen

ban

dab

set

hid

see

Turn to the next page and write them.

Write the words you just read:

1. _____

2. _____

3. _____

4. _____

5. _____

6. _____

7. _____

8. _____

9. _____

10. _____

Turn to the next page.

You did better on that list didn't you? You had the first three or four right with no trouble. You probably broke down after number five but got the last one and maybe even the next to the last. Turn back and check if you wish. Do you have some ideas as to why you did so much better on the second list? We'll check these ideas out with you in a few minutes.

You're ready for your third learning task. Now that you know what is expected, you probably are feeling more comfortable and confident so this time we are going to vary the list. The previous lists have consisted of two consonants with a vowel in between. The next list will have both long words and short words. Read them through once at your regular reading speed and write them on the following page. Ready? Turn the page.

Read the words once.

coat

sweater

hat

gloves

tie

shirt

sox

shoes

jacket

pants

Turn to the next page and write them.

Write the words you just read:

1. _____

2. _____

3. _____

4. _____

5. _____

6. _____

7. _____

8. _____

9. _____

10. _____

Now turn to the next page.

You did very well on that list didn't you? You may have put shirt before tie or shoes before socks but you probably remembered most of the words and your list may have been perfect. Want to turn back and see? It's obvious why this list was easier, isn't it?

Now that you're an experienced "list rememberer" let's give you a really hard one for your final learning task. The list you just learned contained long and short words but they were all nouns. The next list will contain words of different lengths and they will be different parts of speech. Are you up to it? Ready? Turn the page.

Read the words once.

a

boy

went

to

the

grocery

store

to

buy

candy

Turn the page and write these words.

Write the words you remember:

1. _____

2. _____

3. _____

4. _____

5. _____

6. _____

7. _____

8. _____

9. _____

10. _____

Turn to the next page.

You wrote the list perfectly didn't you? This means that: 1) you're an able learner, 2) this book is a successful teacher, and 3) *each list as a learning task has certain properties which almost guarantee errors or success, regardless of the learner* (assuming he could read and had lived in our culture). You were the same learner but you performed with a difference that we could predict even though we didn't know you. Obviously, then each list has some properties which affect the performance of *all* learners.

Let's look at the properties that made us able to predict your performance. By identifying these properties in this simple learning task you will become accustomed to inspecting more complex tasks to determine the presence or absence of these properties and thereby make the performance of your own students more predictable. This knowledge will go far toward making you an increasingly successful teacher for you can remove some of the invisible (but potent!) road blocks to students' learning.

Think back to the first list of nonsense syllables — the one where you didn't do so well. What were the properties of that learning task that made it difficult?

"MEANING!"

You're right, it lacked *meaning* which is probably the single most important factor contributing to successful and rapid learning. *The more meaningful the task, the easier it is to learn.* We all know this. The only thing that is surprising is that in some schools students continue to be presented with meaningless tasks. "Meaning" implies understanding *by the student* not just in the material itself. (All our lists would have been meaningless to a caveman.) We can no longer defend the statement "they just need to be able to do or say it, don't worry if they don't understand it" which has so often been offered as justification for memorization of rote processes in math, names and dates in history, or diagramming sentences. Attempting to have students accomplish a learning task which has little or no meaning is courting academic disaster (to say nothing of ulcers). Before assigning any learning task, the first job of the teacher is to determine whether or not it is meaningful to the learner. If it is not meaningful we need to stop then and there to see if there is any way we can make it more meaningful. This programed book is an attempt to make psychological theory more meaningful to you. You may have been exposed to the same theory in some university or in-service class but our guess is that you only vaguely remember such names as Pavlov and Thorndike. Very little of it had any meaning for your teaching, consequently the material was difficult to learn, you have forgotten most of it, and you don't use it in a deliberate and purposeful way in your daily teaching. By making these learning principles more meaningful we hope you will learn them more easily, remember them longer, and make use of them daily.

Now think back to the second list. It contained the same number of letters, arranged the same way as the first list, a vowel between two consonants. "But they were words," you say. The main difference between a nonsense syllable and a word is that the latter has meaning for the learner, consequently it is easier to learn. Remembering all the words as well as the order of these words gave you some trouble though, didn't it?

Now let's look at the third list:

coat

sweater

hat

gloves

tie

shirt

socks

shoes

jacket

pants

What made this list so much easier to learn? You're right if you thought "They all go together." These words had a great deal of meaning for you because you knew each article and they were all clothing worn by men. Belonging to one category provides meaning over and beyond knowing what each article is. With closer inspection you will find that, not only does the whole list belong to one category, but each pair of words goes together. A coat and sweater are worn on the same part of the body. A hat and gloves cover extremities and are accessories. While you probably remembered most of the words you may have had trouble with the order especially with tie and shirt and socks and shoes as you put them on in an order opposite to the way they were listed. You may have mixed them up because you remembered them in the order you use them. We did that on purpose to point out how typical (and predictable) behavior can interfere with learning.

The last list was a cinch for you because it had maximum meaning. You knew all the words, they were all related to the same idea and they could go together only in a certain order. In fact you didn't even have to remember the order did you? One word just led to another as you remembered the main idea.

From inspection of these lists you see that *meaning* is not a simple property of a learning task which is either present or absent. Meaning exists on a continuum. You can have none at all, a little, a lot, or a tremendous amount. In our lists meaning extended from 1) nonsense syllables with no meaning, 2) words where each one had meaning but there was no meaning in the relationship of one word to another, 3) words where each one represented an article in the category of clothing, and pairs were related one to the other, but there was no reason for the particular order of the pairs, 4) the final list where the words in the sentence were meaningful, each one was related to the word that came before and after it, and the whole group represented an idea.

As a teacher you need to inspect each learning task or assignment to see how you can enhance its meaning. No matter where on the continuum of meaning a task falls, from almost none to a great deal, your job is to see if by connecting it with previous experience, developing order, relationships, or categories, you can increase that meaning and as a result make the learning task easier.

Let's practice doing just that. Suppose you wanted to teach the events that led up to some important historical event such as a discovery, treaty, or war, you would:

a. Teach the most important one first ....Turn to page 35, top
b. Teach the events in the order that they
   occurred ....Turn to page 35, bottom
c. Teach the events in the order in which they
   occurred stressing the factors in each which
   triggered the next ....Turn to page 36
d. Teach the events in the order in which they
   occurred, stressing the factors in each which
   triggered the next event, and relating each
   factor to something in the learner's life which
   helps him understand and categorize that
   event ....Turn to page 37

a. You said you would teach the most important one first.

By doing this, you'll make sure the most important one is remembered. Later in this book you will find out why this is so. Now we need to ask you, what about the other events? How are you going to provide for learning the chain of events, each one of which contributed to the occurrence of the next? Turn back to the question on page 34, and select an answer which will not only provide for the learning of the important ones but their meaning, relationships, and the order of their occurrence as well.

b. You said you would teach the events in the order that they occurred.

You are certainly making it possible for the students to develop the essential relationships, but good teaching not only makes learning possible, it makes it *probable*. Turn back to the question on page 34, and select an answer that shows you are increasing the probability of successful learning by teaching for maximum meaning.

c. You said you would teach the events in the order they occurred, stressing the factors in each which triggered the next.

You are showing good judgment by focusing on the aspects of each event that are relevant to the next event occurring rather than unimportant but vivid elements such as the color of the uniforms, the weapons used, the king's name, or the place the treaty was signed (assuming these were not important). You cannot be sure, however, that these events have real meaning for your learner unless he can see that they are similar to events with which he is already familiar (remember, all our lists were meaningless to cavemen). Your student needs to learn these events are in the same category as something he already knows and understands. Turn back to the question on page 34, and select an answer which will not only develop sequence and relationship but add meaning by categorizing important historical events with meaningful experiences in the learner's life.

d. You said you would teach the events in the order in which they occurred, stressing the factors in each which triggered the next event, and relating each event to something in the learner's life which would help him understand and categorize that event.

You are one in a million! Would that the rest of the teaching profession would do likewise! Helping learners see that being taunted by the winning team makes a difference in their feelings and the way they play the game; and learning that these feelings belong to the same category as the feelings of armies or nations after a crushing defeat will make much of history more meaningful. Likening the events that led up to agreement in the solution of classroom problem to similar events in history, or helping students to see that their "negotiations" with the teacher for a "reasonable" assignment are similar to the negotiations leading to treaties between nations helps learners to better understand national problems with which they can have only vicarious experience. Real understanding can be more readily developed by categorizing important events in history with similar events in the learner's experience. If this is not possible, i.e., he has not experienced something similar (it does not have to be identical), the learning probably cannot have as much depth of meaning. For example, it is almost impossible for a well fed middle class learner to understand poverty except as an unreal Cinderella situation.

While meaning is tremendously important, it is not the only property of a learning task that we need to consider. Sometimes it is very difficult to make learning meaningful, i.e., why you spell a word a certain way. Turn to page 38 to learn about another property of the learning task that you can utilize to propel learning in your classroom.

Sequence of a Learning Task

Let's look once again at the pattern of your learning with the word lists. If we gave you a plus for your correct responses, and you are like most people, your written memory (learning) of the lists would look something like this:

List 1 (Nonsense Syllables)	List 2 (Words)	List 3 (Articles of clothing)	List 4 (Sentence)
1+	1+	1+	1+
2+	2+	2+	2+
3−	3+	3+	3+
4−	4+	4+	4+
5−	5−	5+	5+
6−	6−	6−	6+
7−	7−	7−	7+
8−	8−	8−	8+
9−	9−	9+	9+
10+	10+	10+	10+

Inspecting these patterns should give you some idea of which part of any sequence is the easiest. What part would you predict most people would get right in every list?

The *first part,* of course. Assuming all parts of a task are of equal difficulty, those placed in the first position in any learning sequence are the easiest to learn (very shortly you will find out why). This generalization of *first* position being easiest holds true regardless of the length of the sequence and whether it is *first* position on a list, the *first* part of the period, the *first* part of a day or week, or the *first* in a series of events, words, or numbers. This knowledge should stir your thoughts in terms of what you place *first* (in the day, in spelling, in multiplication, or in a period) from now on. Again we need to remind you that this is based on the assumption "all other things being equal."

Now again inspect the pattern of right and wrong on the lists on page 38. The first position is easiest. What is the next position where you can usually predict correct responses?

Right you are, it's the *last* of any sequence (shortly you'll find the reason for that too). *Assuming all parts of a task are of equal difficulty*, those placed in the *first* position of any sequence are the easiest to learn and those in the *last* position are the next easiest. This does not occur only in our list of words. This same generalization applies to the last thing taught just before lunch, at the end of the day, or at the end of any lesson, whether it be math, reading, or physical education. This knowledge, too, should alert you to factors of position that you can manipulate which you may not have been taking into account as you planned lessons and assignments.

Where do you think you might predict the greatest difficulty of learning in any sequence? To check your prediction, turn back to the lists on page 38 and inspect the typical patterns of responses, to see where most of the errors occurred.

Obviously, the hardest position to learn and remember seems to be *just past the middle*. This generalization holds for any sequence of learning *as long as all parts of the sequence are of comparable difficulty*. Equally obvious is the fact that, if some parts of the sequence are easier than other parts, this generalization will not hold. Had we placed a real word in position six or seven in the list of nonsense syllables, it would have been learned more easily than the nonsense syllable in the last position. Do you remember why?—You're right, it's because the word has more meaning than a nonsense syllable, so that factor compensated for its being placed just past the middle which is the most difficult position in any sequence. Had we printed the sixth or seventh nonsense syllable in purple ink, it, too, would have been easily learned and remembered. Later in this book you'll learn we call such a factor as different color *vividness*. There are many other factors, only one of which is the vividness of a different color ink, which will overcome the problem of a difficult position in a sequence. You will learn about all these factors that help to increase learning as you read this book.

When you teach you need to make sure that you always inspect position in a sequence. Watch out for the learning task that is placed just past the middle of the list of spelling words, in the history lesson, in the list of instructions you give the class, or in anything else you do. If you want to maximize the probability of learning you need to consider whether you should place that task at the beginning or end.

This generalization about importance of position holds true no matter how long or short the sequence is. If we have a hundred items of equal difficulty, obviously the whole list will take much longer, but those items in the 60's or 70's will be the hardest to learn. If you are teaching social studies for a two hour period from 9:00 to 11:00, beware of the time just past the middle, for what you teach from 10:00 to 10:30 is going to be in a position more difficult for students to learn and remember.

There is a reason for the difference of difficulty at different points in a sequence. This reason has been known by psychologists for a long time but has been couched in the psychological jargon of "proactive and retroactive interference" and, as a result, has had little meaning for teachers. Translated into understandable language, it means that each thing you learn can interfere with the next thing you learn (proactive interference), and when you learn the new thing, it can interfere with what you already knew (retroactive interference). This phenomenon is easy to observe if you learn one phone number. This first number is easy to learn but, if you then immediately learn another phone number, some of the numbers of the first are apt to get mixed with the second, i.e., they proactively interfere with the learning of the second number. The minute you learn the second number, you may mix it with or forget the first number, i.e., the second learning retroactively interferes with the first. Drawn in a diagram with the arrows representing interference, a sequence would look like this:

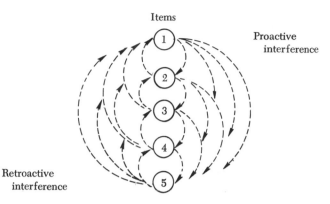

Items

Proactive interference

Retroactive interference

Obviously there is no previous item, so the first item in a series has no proactive interference, therefore it is easiest to learn. The last item in a series has a great deal of proactive interference, but no retroactive interference, because nothing comes after it. As a result, it is easy to remember. As you can see the middle of a series is a snarl of proactive and retroactive interferences and, as a result, this is the position of greatest difficulty with those items coming just after the middle suffering from the snarl that has been accumulated. The longer the list the greater the snarl. Try drawing the lines and arrows in a list of 10 or 20 items and you'll never again work with long sequences all at one time unless they are so meaningful that one leads almost automatically to another as our last list (sentence) did.

Most students have some difficulty learning and remembering the multiplication and division facts. There are many reasons for this but, in your experience, which have you found are the most difficult "time tables" to teach and have students remember? If your experience is like most teachers' you will say the sixes, sevens, or eights. What is the reason for this?

a. The 6's, 7's, and 8's are more difficult than the other multiplication facts .... Turn to page 42, top
b. Usually "time tables" are studies in order from 1 × to 10 × so the 6's, 7's, and 8's are in the most difficult position in the series .... Turn to page 42, bottom
c. There is a backlog of unlearned multiplication facts by the time you get to the 6's, 7's, 8's .... Turn to page 43, top
d. Students have lost their original zest for learning multiplication so they are not trying so hard .... Turn to page 43, bottom

a. You said the 6's, 7's, and 8's are more difficult than the other multiplication facts.

They certainly seem to be more difficult to learn, but why? Why should $3 \times 4 = 12$ be any easier than $3 \times 8 = 24$? And why is 8×3 so much easier to teach than that infernal 8×7 which is missed so often by both children and adults? Turn back to the question on page 41, and select an answer that will explain this phenomenon.

b. You said "time tables" usually are studied in order from $1 \times$ to $10 \times$ so the 6's, 7's, and 8's are in the most difficult position in the series.

How right you are! Most studying is done by going through the series in order and the result is obvious to all of us. What can be done? There are many antidotes to the difficulty of the just-past-the-middle position. Turn to page 44, and you will learn about them.

c. You said there is a backlog of unlearned multiplication facts by the time you get to the 6's, 7's, and 8's.

You're wise to be aware of the fact that we usually proceed too rapidly when we teach the rote part of "memorizing" the multiplication facts. This unlearned "jumble" certainly has an adverse effect. However, usually the 9's and 10's are more easily learned even though there could be an even greater quantity of unlearned facts by the time the 9's are reached. How do you explain that? Turn back to the question on page 41, and select an answer that will explain why we have more trouble with the 7's and 8's than we do with the 9's.

d. You said students have lost their original zest for learning so they aren't trying so hard.

You're wise to know that a student's motivation to learn is one of the most important factors in whether or not he does learn. Yet all students, motivated or otherwise, seem to have trouble with those 6's, 7's, and 8's. Turn back to the question on page 41, and select an answer which will explain why this is so.

While it is not the only possibility, or may at times not be desirable, the simplest solution to learning problems related to position in a sequence is to change that position. This may be accomplished in several ways. One way is to change the position of the just-past-the-middle item so it occurs in either the first or last spot. An example of this might be learning the most difficult word in spelling first, rather than having it in the middle of the list. If this makes a discouraging beginning for apprehensive learners, it might be better to learn the difficult word last. By this procedure the learner may become more sure of himself as he is successful with easier words, and still the difficult word would occupy an easy position (last) in the sequence, as no other spelling word would be learned immediately after it to retroactively interfere with retention of the difficult word.

When the special order of a sequence is essential, such as the procedure for accomplishing a task, a series of directions, or the events that lead up to something, a *second* way of combating the difficulty of the just-past-the-middle problem is to: 1) establish the order of the sequence, 2) pull out the material occupying the just-past-the-middle position, 3) work on it separately and, 4) then replace it in the sequences. An example of this would be establishing the sequence of the eight times tables in one lesson, then in another lesson working on only 7×8 and 8×8 and not working on any other combinations of 8's at this time.

We often use this second procedure in skill learning. A musician establishes the totality of a composition, then works on a passage by itself before he puts it back in sequence in the whole composition. You may work on a single physical skill in golf or diving, such as position of hands or feet, and then put it back into a total movement sequence. A teacher may pull out a certain literary passage for concentrated study and then return so it becomes a part of a larger sequence. She may focus on the "i before e" in "believe." All of these are everyday ways of dealing with the problem of middle position in a sequence.

A learning problem can also arise because certain parts of a composition, word, or skill sequence are more difficult than the rest, but we need to make sure the learning problem is not also the result of that learning occurring just past the middle of a sequence.

"Chaining" is another technique of teaching that takes advantage of the first position in a series being the easiest. It is often used when the order of a sequence is important as an end product but the order is not essential in learning. Many foreign language phrases or automatic sequences of physical skills fall in this category. In chaining, the last item of the sequence is taught first. It is easy to learn because there is only one item and it is in first learning position. Then the next to last item is added in front of the last item. Then the third from the last item is added to the front of the chain. By adding to the front, the new item to be learned is always in that optimal first position while the items already learned occupy more difficult positions, but they also receive more practice.

The technique of chaining is often used to get correct repetition or pronunciation of phrases in foreign language instruction and is known as "backward buildup." "Cómo está usted?", we could begin by having the learner say "usted." Then we would add "está usted" and, finally, "Cómo está usted?" Another example would be learning the final syllable of a word that is difficult to pronounce, then adding the syllable just in front of it, and continuing to add syllables until you have the whole word. (If you have trouble saying "tachistascope" try "scope" then say "a-scope" then "kiss-t-scope," then "tachista-scope." Soon you will have no more problem.) Try this technique the next time you have difficulty with a sequence such as a musical phrase or memorizing something. Just the vividness of doing something differently will help. Obviously this type of learning is not possible when the second item in the sequence can only occur after the first is completed as in doing a long division problem or reading for meaning. Chaining has not been used by many teachers but it is an interesting and effective technique when appropriately employed.

A *fourth* way of overcoming positional difficulty is by learning something in sequence and then at the end reviewing the specific, just-past-in-the-middle part, thereby placing it in the last position which makes it easier to remember. Suppose you were giving this set of directions, "Today we are going to work on using descriptive words so the reader has a better picture of the event we are describing. Read the chapter about Daniel Boone. Imagine you were with him and write a story about what happened to you on a day of the expedition. Use words that help the reader see what you saw and feel as you felt. Use your dictionary or signal me if you need help. We will work for about 30 minutes." To put the important direction about using descriptive words in the last position, you would give the sequence of directions and then conclude with, "Remember we are going to use descriptive words that will help the reader feel as if he were experiencing himself the things we saw and the way we felt."

We need to point out that the examples in this book are merely illustrations not "how-you-ought-to-do-it recipes." Most real learning situations are infinitely more complex, but it helps to see and understand a generalization in a simple and obvious form before we begin to incorporate it in our plans for more complex learning situations.

A *fifth* solution to the just-past-the-middle snarl could be to break the learning task into smaller parts so the length of each sequence is shortened, thereby eliminating so much serial interference. As a sequence becomes longer, the interference problems compound. This is easy to see if you imagine yourself learning three phone numbers. Suppose it takes you one minute each to remember them perfectly. Now imagine yourself learning a sequence of 30 phone numbers. You'd never be able to do it in 30 minutes and remember all of them correctly and in the right order. As the sequence becomes longer, problems from interference increase exponentially.

This knowledge of compounding proactive and retroactive interference should help you resist the temptation to give long assignments, especially when the elements of the task are the same, such as 50 similar math problems or 100 spelling words. Even if your motives are so noble as to keep the group busy and "out of your hair" so you have time to help each individual, you are probably encouraging learning snarls and the practice of errors.

We should surely keep these problems of length of sequence in mind as we assign 20 spelling words or ten multiplication facts. Far better that we work on a few at a time, not moving to the next group until these are well learned.

Whole vs Part Learning

Thinking about how much to assign at one time, brings us to the important question of *whole* versus *part* learning. When is it more efficient to work with the whole task and when is it more efficient to break it into parts? Again it will help to look back at your learning task of the lists of words. (In this book we are trying to use your own learning experience to make psychological generalizations more meaningful so that they will be easier for you to learn and remember.) Think back to the list of nonsense syllables. If you were responsible for teaching any six-year-old to say them, how many would you work with at one time?

a. One ....Turn to page 48, top
b. Two or three ....Turn to page, 48, bottom
c. Five or six ....Turn to page 49, top
d. All of them ....Turn to page 49, bottom

a. You said you would work with one nonsense syllable at a time.

This would be a good idea if you were working with a two- or three-year-old, for first he might need to learn to say each sound correctly before he could put the sounds together in sequence. Sometimes even adults do this when they are trying to learn a word like "tachistascope." They might first say only "chis" (the most difficult because it's in the middle) and then put the "ta" and "tascope" fore and aft. With six-year-olds, however, they probably could learn more than one nonsense syllable at a time, and if you began with more than one, it would be more efficient. It would also be easier for them to learn the order of the syllables, for each time, they would be practicing some of the order of the sequence. Turn back to the question on page 47, and select an answer that would make the learning task efficient as well as easy.

b. You said you would work with two or three nonsense syllables at a time.

You are a mighty efficient teacher and we predict you will be successful. It is possible for most six-year-olds to handle a series such as "kef, lak, mil," or if that is too hard just "kef, lak." In this way, not only are you teaching the sounds, but you are teaching the position of one in relation to the other so the order doesn't have to be learned later. Now let's see how you would work with a different kind of list. Turn to page 50.

c. You said you would work with five or six nonsense syllables at one time.

We wish you luck, and you'll need it because it will probably take a great deal longer for your six-year-old to learn those big chunks than it would if you took smaller "bites" of learning. The words that are fourth and fifth in your series of six are sure to get "braided" with others before they are finally learned. Turn back to the question on page 47, and choose an answer that will eliminate some of this undesirable interference.

d. You said you would teach all of the nonsense syllables at one time.

You must be kidding! We don't believe you really chose this; you're only reading it to see what we have to say. You certainly know better than to assign a long list of nonsense syllables, but what about those long lists of spelling words, multiplication facts, names and dates that are often assigned at school? This is just as inexcusable as it would be if you really had chosen this answer. Turn back to the right answer to the question on page 47, reread that answer so it occupies the last position in your mind and you'll remember to assign small amounts when material is not meaningful to the learner. (Better that you don't assign meaningless material at all but rather figure out a way to make it meaningful.)

You have learned that, when you work with material that has no built in order or meaning, you had better take it in small learning "bites." Now what about material that has much meaning and order? Think about the last list "a boy went to the grocery store to buy candy." How much of that list would you try to teach at one time to a six-year-old?

a. One or two words .... Turn to page 51, top
b. Three or four words .... Turn to page 51, bottom
c. Six or seven words .... Turn to page 52, top
d. All of them .... Turn to page 52, bottom

a. You said you would teach one or two words at a time.

The six-year-old probably would feel insulted because you thought he couldn't learn more than "a boy" and "went to" at one time. You are reasonably sure he could work faster than that. Besides you are losing important meaning and relationship as you chop the sentence into such small pieces. Turn back to the question on page 50, and choose an answer that won't waste any of his (and your) time.

b. You said you would teach three or four words at one time.

You are using good judgment if you break it up into the meaningful units of "a boy went" "to the grocery store" "to buy candy." This would be just right if you were working with a very young child or one who was learning to speak English. Our guess is that the average six-year-old would not need to work with such small pieces. Besides, breaking it up actually diminishes meaning of the whole idea. Turn back to the question on page 50, and select an answer that will take into account the language learning ability possessed by most six-year-olds.

c. You said you would teach six or seven words at a time.

This would be a good idea if you taught "a boy went to the grocery store" and then taught "to buy candy." We don't believe, however, that "to buy candy" is so difficult that it needs to be taught separately so why waste the time doing it? Turn back to the question on page 50, and select the answer that will make the best use of time for you and the six-year-old.

d. You said you would teach all of the words at one time.

And a wise decision that is! You are enhancing meaning by keeping the whole idea together. "a boy went to the grocery store to buy candy," actually has a great deal more meaning than "a boy went" or "to buy candy" when those phrases are by themselves. Most six-year-olds are capable of learning those ten words with no trouble at all because the idea has so much meaning for them. Knowing that you assign small amounts of a meaningless list and the whole sentence if it is meaningful, what would you now say is the important generalization about whole versus part learning? Really think about it before you read the next page to see if you are right.

For efficiency in learning you work with the smallest amounts possible without sacrificing maximum meaning or wasting time.

In the list of nonsense syllables you could work with only one and not lose meaning but you are wasting time if the learner can deal with more than one at a time (and a six-year-old can). If you were teaching a much younger child, you probably would need to work with one at a time so he could learn to make the correct sound before he tried to put parts of the series together. In the list which is a sentence, when you separate the words you are actually destroying meaning because no part has as much meaning as the whole idea.

Spelling presents a situation similar to our second list of unrelated words, for most spelling lists have very little meaning one word to the other. Even though they belong to the same category (families of words ran, fan, can), or words that are examples of the same phoneme-grapheme correspondence (phone, phosphorous, phonics), it is usually more effective to work on only a few words at a time. With a young child you would work on only one or two words. An older learner may be able to work on more, but at no time should he study (for the first time) 10 or 20 at a sitting. A half hour to study spelling is usually five to ten minutes of learning and 20 to 25 minutes of proactive and retroactive interference, at best just wasted time, but more often actually destructive learning experience.

In our so called "drill" periods in arithmetic we often commit the same error. Once a learner has seen the progressive relationship of his "time tables," he has perceived the meaning. Now, to translate his knowledge into an automatic response, he needs to work with less than 10 combinations at a time. Perhaps he could work on the first five. Then *after* he knows those, he could learn the six and seven combinations. After he has learned those, he is ready to learn his eight and nine combinations. Testing a learner on 100 combinations and then telling him to learn all he doesn't know is not only an inexcusable teaching blunder but an insurmountable learning task for most students. Of course if he already knows all but three of them, those three would be an appropriate assignment.

What about material where there is more meaning in the relationship of one part to another than there is in any one of those parts alone? A boy going to a grocery store to buy candy has more meaning than just the word "boy," "store" or "candy." As a result, breaking that sentence into parts destroys some of its meaning so we teach it all together. Again, when we're teaching a very young child we would probably break it up into meaningful phrases, because he couldn't remember it all at once and it really wouldn't have so much meaning as a whole for him.

If we were working on a poem, we would go through the whole poem to develop maximum meaning, then work on one or two lines at a time provided we weren't destroying meaning. If we were losing meaning, we would need to take more lines or a stanza. As we teach a mathematical operation like long division, we need to develop first the concept of division. Without this there will be no meaning. To increase understanding, we should then work on the whole operation with concrete representation. Only after this is understood should we break it into the component steps of division, multiplication, subtraction, and "bring down." Much of the confusion in mathematics is that a well meaning but uninformed teacher has taught only the sequence of separate steps in an operation, thinking that made it simpler. As a result, meaning was sacrificed and learning became more difficult.

Focusing in great depth on one fact or event in history without developing relationship to prior and following events constitutes the same error in part-versus-whole decisions in teaching. Once the meaning has been established however, it is wise to take a small chunk and work in depth. We should work on the details of the voyage of the Mayflower only after its relationship to prior and subsequent events has been established.

Having determined that we will work on the *smallest part that will maintain meaning and yet not waste the learner's time* (obviously it's inefficient for a 12-year-old to get out his pencil, paper, and book to learn one spelling word and then put all the material away), how do we ensure that the learning is accomplished?

"Practice," you say, and in some cases you would be right but in other cases you would be wrong. Want us to prove it? All right, take out your pencil and write that first list of nonsense syllables (no fair looking back).

1. _____

2. _____

3. _____

4. _____

5. _____

6. _____

7. _____

8. _____

9. _____

10. _____

Now write the last list, the one that made a sentence.

1. _____

2. _____

3. _____

4. _____

5. _____

6. _____

7. _____

8. _____

9. _____

10. _____

Well, what do you know? Even after your seeing it, reading about it, and working with it, you still don't know the first list, do you? But you could have written the last one without ever seeing it, or our mentioning it again. You've had the same amount of practice on both lists but you know one and not the other. How do you account for this?

You're absolutely right, the difference is *meaning*. If you have enough meaning you won't need practice. Let us give you an example. Look at this number 13975. It probably doesn't mean anything to you so you would need to spend some time practicing if you were to remember it a month from now. Suppose, however, we told you that by reading this book you would receive a salary increase of $139.75 per month. Our guess is that we would have to tell you only once and a month from now you would remember how much should be added to your pay check.

If you remember only one thing after reading this book, we hope it will be that *by making learning meaningful you can reduce the amount of time you need to spend in practice*. This knowledge will make it well worth the time you have spent in reading, to say nothing of saving energy and countless hours for you and your students in the classroom.

There are several other factors, however, that also can reduce the time necessary for practice. These factors in learning are *vividness, motivation, reinforcement, feeling tones, active participation, knowl-*

edge of results, degree of guidance, and transfer. Many of these do not have much meaning for you now, so we don't expect you to remember them until we have made them more meaningful.

No one of these factors is always the most important but they vary depending on the learner, the learning task, and the learning environment. Even though they operate together, we'll talk about each of them separately so it will become a meaningful (and we hope much used) part of your repertoire of daily teaching skills.

Vividness

Vividness refers to the ability of something to attract your attention. This is usually because it is different from what you are currently experiencing, what you are used to, or what you expected. If we had printed the seventh word in our list of nonsense syllables in a different color ink or used a different type of print, you probably would have remembered it even though it was in the most difficult position (just past the middle).

The Brain Institute at UCLA has demonstrated that anything novel or different elicits an alerting reflex in our brain and causes us to attend to the different thing rather than that to which we have been attending. This discovery in brain research comes as no surprise to a teacher who thought she was teaching a fascinating lesson until a bee flew into the classroom. The first appearance of the Beatles' hairdo, psychedelic colors, or mini skirts caused the same alerting or "attending" reaction.

Nothing remains novel or different, however, for after we see it for a while we get used to it and habituation sets in so we no longer attend to it. The roar of a jet plane flying low over a school will cause students to look up, but students in schools that are located in airport landing patterns aren't even aware of the noise when they are working. If our entire list of nonsense syllables had been printed in red ink, it would have had no effect, for nothing would have been different.

How do you apply this information about the alerting reflex to daily classroom teaching? You simply inspect a learning task to see if you need to increase its vividness by adding interest, novelty, or something different. Just moving to a different teaching position at the side or back of the room, using color, changing the schedule, making a game of learning, lowering your voice, all of these will elicit the alerting reflex of your students.

Have you ever lost your voice and had to conduct your class in a whisper, writing directions on the board? Usually the students are wonderful, exceptionally quiet, and you have a great day. We would like to believe it was because the learners were so considerate of your condition. Unfortunately, however, if your voice problem continues, you will learn that it was because of the differentness of the situation, and all too soon habituation sets in, they become their old selves, and you decide to stay home until your voice returns and you can again conduct class.

Novelty or differentness does not have to be extreme to attract a student's attention. We are *not* suggesting you employ a lot of gimmicks or hang by your heels from the ceiling in order to alert your students to the fact that there is something they should learn. Also, if you never do things the same way, routine itself becomes novel and doing things the same way becomes something different. You shouldn't expend a great deal of energy thinking of a "gimmick" but when learning is slowing down, or routine becomes boring, just a little vividness can revive the attending behavior of your students.

Suppose you are having a difficult time trying to get students to write carefully and hand in neat papers? What's "suppose" about that you ask? We know it's a horrendous problem in every classroom. You wish to add vividness to focus their attention on the appearance and legibility of their papers. Should you:

a. Hand out a mimeographed assignment with cross outs, smears, illegible words, run together sentences and announce that anyone who didn't complete it correctly will have to stay after school? .... Turn to page 59
b. Put a cartoon of your smiling face on the neat papers and your frowning scowl on the sloppy ones, then return them to your students? .... Turn to page 60
c. Announce the names of students who had neat papers and say they are excused from any writing assignments for the rest of the week because they obviously know how to do a good paper? .... Turn to page 61
d. Tape a piece of candy on the neat papers, handing them back with the announcement that those students had given you a "treat" with such neat papers, now you were returning the favor? .... Turn to page 62

a. **You said you would hand out a mimeographed assignment with cross outs, smears, illegible words, run together sentences and announce that anyone who didn't complete it correctly will have to stay after school.**

We bet you had a hard time selecting the answer to this question because every answer added vividness to the learning task. You could not know which one was the best solution without knowing the situation, so you couldn't judge which would be the most appropriate for a particular group of learners. We are adding vividness to this question because all four answers are correct. You are accustomed to having only one right answer so we have attracted your attention (elicited your alerting reflex) by providing no wrong answers. We hope the novelty of this will help you learn about vividness so we don't need to practice with any more questions about it. If we made this experience different enough, you will learn to incorporate vividness in your own teaching and will have had enough practice by answering only one question. Turn now to page 63.

b. You said put line drawings of smiling faces on the neat papers and frowns on the sloppy ones and return them to your students.

We bet you had a hard time selecting the answer to this question because every answer added vividness to the learning task. You could not know which one was the best solution without knowing the situation, so you couldn't judge which would be the most appropriate for a particular group of learners. We are adding vividness to this question because all four answers are correct. You are accustomed to having only one right answer so we have attracted your attention (elicited your altering reflex) by providing no wrong answers. We hope the novelty of this will help you learn about vividness so we don't need to practice with any more questions about it. If we made this experience different enough, you will learn to incorporate vividness in your own teaching and you will have had enough practice by answering only one question. Turn to page 63.

c. You would announce the names of students who had neat papers and say they are excused from any writing assignments for the rest of the week because they obviously know how to do a good paper.

We bet you had a hard time selecting the answer to this question because every answer added vividness to the learning task. You could not know which one was the best solution without knowing the situation, so you couldn't judge which would be the most appropriate for a particular group of learners. We are adding vividness to this question because all four answers are correct. You are accustomed to having only one right answer so we have attracted your attention (elicited your alerting reflex) by providing no wrong answers. We hope the novelty of this will help you learn about vividness so we don't need to practice with any more questions about it. If we made this experience different enough, you will learn to incorporate vividness in your own teaching and you will have had enough practice by answering only one question. Turn now to page 63.

d. You would tape a piece of candy on the neat papers handing them back with the announcement that those students had given you a "treat" with such neat papers, now you are returning the favor.

We bet you had a hard time selecting the answer to this question because every answer added vividness to the learning task. You would not know which one was the best solution without knowing the situation, so you couldn't judge which would be the most appropriate for a particular group of learners. We are adding vividness to this question because all four answers are correct. You are accustomed to having only one right answer so we have attracted your attention (elicited your alerting reflex) by providing no wrong answers. We hope the novelty of this will help you learn about vividness so we don't need to practice with any more questions about it. If we made this experience different enough, you will learn to incorporate vividness in your own teaching and you will have had enough practice by answering only one question. Turn to page 63.

Degree of Guidance

How much should a teacher help or guide a learner? Under what condition is this guidance facilitating to learning and when should the teacher withdraw help so dependency is not fostered, rather independence in learning is increased? Are these conditions related to the differentness in learners or to the different kinds of learning tasks? These are tremendously important questions to which every teacher needs answers if he or she is to maximize students' learning.

We emphasized at the beginning of this book the continuous relationship between the learner, his learning task, and his teacher's actions. Only for purposes of *your* learning are we temporarily separating these aspects so we can focus more intently on the properties of each which can be utilized to increase the speed and amount of learning.

Obviously the amount of guidance a learner needs is partially related to his own personality make up. Some students need reassurance and support almost every step of the way. Others are comfortable proceeding independently and have little need for support. A detailed personality inventory of each student is not necessary, for we can separate the "one from the other" by careful observation of the *quality of his performance* with and without guidance. In this way we find out who needs increased support and guidance, and who doesn't. As a result, we expend our teaching energy where it is needed rather than waste it where it is not necessary or may even become an interference to learning. On the basis of personality factors this decision of how much help to give must be made for each learner as a result of our observation and knowledge about him.

There is, however, a psychological generalization which applies to *all* learners and is related to the learning task. *At the initial stages of any learning task, wise teacher guidance will greatly increase the rate and degree of that learning. As a student gains proficiency with a particular learning, guidance should be withdrawn gradually so the student learns to depend on himself and is able to function without guidance.* If we think about it, this is only common sense. If we wish to learn something entirely new, we'll learn faster if we get some expert help at the beginning. After we begin to be comfortable with our new learning we need to work on our own to become proficient.

This generalization of *maximum guidance at the initial stages* of each new learning and then *gradual withdrawal of guidance* enables us as teachers to program our educational energy more productively. If we explain a new process to a group of learners, we had better not leave them alone to "work on what you have learned." We need to circulate among them so they will have help available when they need it and will not be practicing mistakes. If we really want students to work independently, it had better be on something where they are far enough along in their learning so that we may justifiably and productively remove our guidance.

The current practice of assigning lower pupil loads to primary teachers is based on the premise that younger children are at the initial stages of learning in more areas and therefore need more teacher guidance. An upper grade teacher could justifiably argue, however, that when older students are at initial stages of learning (decimal fractions, parts of a sentence, foreign language) those students also need maximum guidance. One advantage (among many) of team teaching is that it is possible to adjust pupil teacher ratio to accommodate the need for maximum guidance at the initial stages of any new learning for any age learner.

Suppose you had decided to introduce a new skill or concept to your total class. To provide appropriate help after you had introduced the skill you would need to:

a. Give the whole class a practice period immediately following the introduction of the new material. . . . . Turn to page 65, top
b. Divide the class into groups according to their ability with the new learning (not their general ability) and let them all practice at various levels of difficulty. . . . . Turn to page 65, bottom
c. Divide the class into groups according to their ability with the new learning, have one group practice with your help and supervision while the other groups work on a skill (related if possible) which they can do independently but need to practice . . . . Turn to page 66, top
d. Work with the total class a few more times before they begin independent practice. . . . . Turn to page 66, bottom

a. You said you would give the whole class a practice period immediately following the introduction of the new material.

We're glad you know that students need to practice a new skill and that they usually don't learn it from one introductory lesson. You're giving yourself a rough job however, for almost all of them are going to need your supervision and help so there won't be enough of you to go around. As a result, there is going to be a lot of wasted time and frustration as each one who needs you has to wait his turn. You have learned that you can anticipate almost all students need guidance at an initial phase of learning, so make life easier for yourself and more satisfactory for your students by turning back to the question on page 64, and selecting an answer where there will be enough of you to meet your students' needs.

b. You said you would divide the class into groups according to their ability in the new learning (not their general ability) and let them all practice at various levels of difficulty.

We're delighted that you know your students will vary in their ability in the new learning and that you have the wisdom to adjust the practice task accordingly. If the practice in the new material is so easy that they can do it with no help, they won't learn very much for they already know it. If it is at the appropriate level of difficulty, they will probably need your guidance and help because they will be at an initial stage in their learning. There is only one of you and many of them so you'll never be able to get around to everyone who needs you. Use your good idea of assessing the ability of your learners, turn back to the question on page 64, and select an answer that won't kill you off.

c. You said you would divide the class into groups according to their ability with the new learning, have one group practice with your help and supervision while the other groups work on a skill (related if possible) which they can do independently but need to practice.

You are a gifted teacher! And because you have sense enough to know you can't help everyone at the same time, you'll live a lot longer. Teachers, not so wise as you, give the whole class a new kind of follow-up or have everyone start a new project and then wonder why they are exhausted and the students frustrated. You are probably astute enough to begin practice with your most able learners in this particular skill because they will quickly progress through the initial stages where they need your guidance and soon become independent, freeing you to work with students who will need your help for a longer period of time. The slower students can begin with easy assignments and related activities, but if you follow the principles of learning outlined in this book they also *should be able to achieve proficiency and independence.* They will take a little longer to get through the initial stage of learning, and your presence and guidance will insure that they do! You're a gifted student because you didn't take long to get through the initial stage of learning this generalization. You need no further guidance, so turn to page 67.

d. You said you would work with the total class a few more times before they began independent practice.

At least you have sense enough not to turn them all loose to practice at the same time when, because they are in the initial stage of learning, they will all need your help. However, you may be under-estimating some of them who are ready to start working without additional total class instruction. Turn back to the question on page 64, and select an answer that reflects your knowledge that you can't help all of them at the same time, but that you will "get those going" who are ready.

Positive and Negative Transfer

What accounts for that difference between a fast and a slow learner in a new activity? I.Q. (which is a learner's "horsepower" or rate of learning) can account for some of that difference, but learning that has been already accomplished in the past may account for a great deal more. These old learnings *transfer* into and propel the new learning. The psychological term for this is *positive transfer*.

Let's look at the example of a physical activity, swimming. We see three swimmers the same size, age, and general physical coordination go to a pool with a competent instructor. Not one of them can swim at the beginning of instruction. Their need for guidance at this initial phase of instruction is obvious. To shove them into the pool, direct them to learn to swim, and leave them without guidance is surely courting disaster. Some of our academic fatalities result from just such procedure where a student is "in over his head" in some subject and no help is available.

We will probably see a different performance in each of our young swimmers. Let's assume one boy learns very rapidly, one in about the normal time, and the third has a terribly difficult time learning. Why? Natural aptitude for swimming? Not necessarily.

Further investigation could reveal that the rapid learner had lived near the beach. While he didn't learn to swim he played in the water. He held on to floats and kicked and splashed his feet. He held his breath, put his face in the water, and opened his eyes to look under the surface, coming up for air when he needed it. To teach him to swim, the instructor helped him coordinate all these past learnings, use his arms appropriately, and away he went. The positive transfer from his past learning accounted for the speed of his present learning.

The typical learner possessed none of these past learnings. The instructor had to teach him to feel comfortable in the water, kick his feet and move his arms appropriately, not breathe when his face was in the water but when it came out. There was no old learning to transfer into the new skill of swimming so it took more time to learn all these skills and then coordinate them. There was no previous learning, however, which interfered with this new learning so he learned to swim in the usual amount of time.

The slow learner, when younger, had been pushed into a pool and nearly drowned, consequently he had a great fear of water. He

67

could not use his arms and legs well because they were tense and rigid. Each time he got his face wet he panicked and moved his head out of the water so he was not able to learn to breathe correctly. He held on to the sides so he could not get the feel of the water supporting his body. When he got water in his eyes, he squeezed them shut until he could wipe them. Consequently, he could not see where he was going. All of this frightened him more. These responses which were learned from his previous experience were interfering with and inhibiting his new learning. The psychological label for this interference is *negative transfer*.

The term *positive transfer* implies that past learnings are aiding or propelling new learning. *Negative transfer* implies that past learnings are actively interfering with the accomplishment of a new learning. This psychological generalization about transfer of learning is a very important one, for we as teachers must scrutinize a learning task to see which past learnings could assist the accomplishment of the new learning and which past learnings may interfere with that new learning. As much as possible we should utilize any past learning of the student which will yield positive transfer. We should beware of or eliminate interference from any past learning that may negatively transfer. This is one reason it is important to give maximum guidance at the initial stages of learning. If you learn something incorrectly, that error will negatively transfer and interfere as you try to relearn correctly. Have you ever learned the incorrect pronunciation of a word? You know how hard you have to focus when you say the word to keep the incorrect sound from automatically coming out. Placing your hands incorrectly on golf clubs, learning to play music with some errors in tempo, learning to do a careless job, all make the learning of the correct response more difficult. The old habits negatively transfer and interfere with learning the correct (and new) response.

As we teach, we must be alert to the kinds of learning which will positively transfer into and thereby facilitate the new learning. "Learning how to learn" has become an important objective for students because this is a learning that will positively transfer into every new learning situation.

Most learning objectives are more restricted in their possibility for transfer. For example: knowing how to bake a chocolate cake will provide positive transfer in learning how to bake other kinds of cakes, muffins, biscuits, or even waffles. It won't help a bit when you get ready to broil a steak, but your knowledge of using the oven will. In the same way your knowledge of mathematics will positively transfer to propel your learning in statistics, engineering, drafting, or budgeting. Math may not provide positive transfer in sociology or medicine but your ability to read tables, graphs, and charts will.

As we consciously inspect a new learning task to see what learning in the student's past will provide positive transfer, we are often amazed at how much we find. Teaching divisions of fractions would not be so difficult if the teacher used the student's knowledge of division of whole numbers to assist his learning (and understanding!) $1/2 \overline{\smash{)}7/8} =$.

In order to encourage positive transfer we bring the old and new learning together and stress the similarities. For example, we have the student focus on the learning that $2\overline{\smash{)}10}$ means how many pairs or groups of 2 are contained in 10? How many pairs of stockings could you make out of 10 stockings? Then we would parallel that example $1/2\overline{\smash{)}7/8}$ which means how many halves are contained in 7/8 of something. How many half pies are in 7/8 of a pie? The answer 1 3/4 becomes meaningful as the student sees one half of the whole pie and 3/4 of another half of a whole pie are contained in 7/8 of a whole pie in the same way that 5 pairs of stockings are contained in 10 stockings.

To increase positive transfer we need to bring the old and new learning together so students see the similarity between what they know and what they need to learn. $1/2\overline{\smash{)}7/8}$ and $2\overline{\smash{)}10}$.)

Unfortunately the opposite transfer (negative) frequently occurs as the student's past experience of cutting something *in* half, or dividing *by* 2, provides negative transfer that interferes with dividing *by* a half. (They think that 7/8 divided *by* 1/2 means 7/8 cut *in* half.)

To use another example, if the learner understands, rather than has merely memorized that $4 \times 8 = 32$ and $32 + 32 = 64$, this understanding will transfer into $8 \times 8 = 64$. He'll understand the numerical relationship and remember the combination longer than if he merely memorized 8×8 without any "assist" (positive transfer) from what he already knows.

Conversely, if he learns $8 \times 8 = 64$, we want to stay away from $9 \times 7 = 63$ for a while because we want no confusion (negative transfer) between the similarity of 64 and 63 to occur. In order to avoid negative transfer we need to keep the old and new learnings apart. It will help to think of learnings as wet paint. If you want two learnings to run together (positive transfer), bring them together side by side. If you don't want them to run together because you'll achieve a muddy hue (learning confusion), keep them apart. "Clear as mud" could mean the new learning is not understood because we have some negative transfer from some old learning. Only *if there already is confusion* do we bring the two learnings together to straighten it out by pointing out the difference. For example, the confusion may exist between "their" and "there," or dividing *by* one half and dividing in half or by two. If there is negative transfer or confusion, we need to help a student see how each one is different so he can look for the appropriate cues to tell them apart. It is as if you met one twin and got to know her very well. When you later met her twin sister, you probably would not confuse her with your old friend even though they were very similar. Knowing one thing well prevents confusing it with another. Only if you got them mixed would you need to stand the twins side by side to look for distinguishing features such as a freckle, different hair line, or wider eyebrows, so you could use this cue to tell them apart.

You will notice that the examples in the book are designed to bring to mind something you already know or have experienced to facilitate your learning (positive transfer) of the new ideas presented. You assist your own learning as you recall what you know from psychology classes plus your own teaching experience and apply that knowledge to assist your learning of new material in this book. At the same time you are also experiencing a great deal of interference from negative transfer for you may have to adjust some of your old habits and platitudes ("give 'em lots of practice," "a low I.Q. can't learn," "it's the kid's or his parents' fault if he doesn't learn," "forget theory and start teaching") which by now you should know can be incorrect statements.

Let's see which has taken over in your learning, positive or negative transfer as you complete this statement. The best way to group students for instruction is:

a. by I.Q. ....Turn to page 71, top
b. by reading ability..................Turn to page 71, bottom
c. by random grouping......................Turn to page 72
d. by an analysis (or estimate) of factors they possess which will contribute to the *specific* learning objectives to be accomplished in a particular lesson...............Turn to page 73

70

a. You said you would group students for instructions by I.Q.

A lot of people (people you understand, *not* educators) have done just that. Their decision is the result of negative transfer from the erroneous notion that I.Q. is the most important factor in achievement. We now know better. I.Q. would predict the rate of accomplishment in some brand new learning for which there would be no possibility of positive or negative transfer. There are few learnings like this. Consequently, anyone who still groups *only* by I.Q. needs theirs examined. If you are reading this we suspect it is only because you are curious about what we have to say to such a response. Turn back quickly to page 70, and select a better answer.

b. You said you would group learners for instruction by reading ability.

That would be a good idea if success with the particular lesson was dependent only on the students' ability to read the specific material. Sometimes this is true, but unless the actual objective is only reading graded material, we need to consider other factors. Often reading is merely a means to get information which could also be secured from a film, diagram, or teacher. You can understand all kinds of subjects: math, history, geography, sociology (need we go on?), even if you don't read about them. Most of your understanding of space exploration and the problem of putting a man on the moon is a result of your listening and looking at T.V., not from reading books on astro physics. Give up? Then turn back to the question on page 70, and select an answer that shows you are thinking about what you have just read and are not having trouble from the negative transfer of past platitudes or erroneous practice.

c. You said you would group learners for instruction by random grouping.

At least nobody could hold you accountable for using the wrong variable in grouping, and we admire your willingness to work with a wide range of ability. It's going to be tough though, for you're going to be like the swimming instructor. Some students will flourish as positive transfer propels their learning. Some will do all right and some will have trouble. You'll be in the latter category for you'll be stuck with trying to make wise teaching decisions for all three types at the same time. Turn back to the question on page 70, and select an answer that shows your learning from reading this book is positively transferring into your answer to the question.

d. You said you would group learners for instruction by an analysis (or estimate) of factors they possess which will contribute to the specific learning objective to be accomplished.

Hooray for your positive transfer! You indeed have eliminated the negative transfer from all the platitudes you have heard about *one* best way of grouping. How you group depends on what you are trying to accomplish educationally and the knowledge of the student that is relevant to that accomplishment. If you want students to learn to change a carburetor, it's obvious that their previous experience with machines and their manual dexterity are more relevant than their reading ability or I.Q. If you want them to learn Algebra II, their performance in Algebra I is relevant for it will provide positive transfer into new algebraic learning. An I.Q. of 190 or a super reader who has never had the mathematical background would be lost. If your objective is to encourage students to use reading as a leisure activity, you could group by interest in particular kinds of literature (*not* the "fairy tale-ers" with the "science fictioners"). The best readers in the class will not fall into the same interest group nor will all the slow readers. Probably you will have a full range of reading ability and I.Q. in each group, but they will be a teachable group because they're all interested in the same thing. Obviously, if you had a completely new learning, Berber or Sanskrit for example, you might assess the learner's aptitude for learning language and not depend so much on positive transfer from previous learnings (except linguistic knowledge). Learning psychological generalizations is not a completely new learning to you, however. By choosing this answer you show you have read carefully and have not let previous erroneous educational platitudes negatively transfer into and interfere with your present learnings, so you are ready to turn to page 74.

You have covered many psychological generalizations so far in this book. We are just past the middle of your sequence of learning, so we are concerned that we don't commit the positional error about which we cautioned you. (Remember your difficulty in those word lists?) To avoid that just-past-the-middle sag let's review what we have talked about.

One of the best ways to review is by "highly motivated practice." This is another name for a test. It is "practice," for you are reviewing and using what you have learned. It is "highly motivated" because most of us really try to do well on a test. We don't half-way read or think about other things while we're answering questions on a test but we may engage in these side activities if we are in a normal study situation. The only bad aspect of using a test as motivated practice is that it may generate too much anxiety. We are eliminating that possibility, for no one but you will know which items you get right or wrong. This knowledge should help you focus on that which you still need to learn, so you will not waste time on the parts you already know.

All set for your "motivated practice"?

Read the next page.

Mark the following true (T) or false (F)

_____ 1. Teaching is a learned skill.

_____ 2. Knowledge of content is more important than methodology.

_____ 3. Knowledge of how to teach is more important than knowledge of subject matter.

_____ 4. "Meaning" of a learning task is one of the most important factors in successful learning.

_____ 5. "Meaning" is either present or absent in an assignment.

_____ 6. First position is the easiest learning position in a sequence.

_____ 7. Last position in a sequence is easy to learn.

_____ 8. Just past the middle is the most difficult position in a learning sequence.

_____ 9. Because something is just past the middle in a sequence, it need not be difficult to learn.

_____10. It is always better to learn the whole than just a part.

_____11. To really learn something you must practice it.

_____12. To increase learning you must have more time.

_____13. You can reduce the amount of time needed in learning by adding vividness.

_____14. Younger children need more teacher guidance than older ones.

_____15. I.Q. is the most important factor in learning.

_____16. Transfer from old learnings always aids new learning.

_____17. If you wish to avoid negative transfer keep the two learnings separate.

Turn to the next page to check your answers. If you miss any, reread the pages indicated by the answer *before* you go on to the new material. The practice (rereading) will go far toward helping you remember the correct answer. Going back and learning what you don't know before going on will make a shorter and therefore easier sequence of learning.

1. True — page 1

2. False — page 2

3. False — page 2

4. True — page 31

5. False — page 33

6. True — page 38

7. True — page 39

8. True — page 39

9. True — page 40 (plus all the other factors in learning)

10. False — page 47

11. False — page 56

12. False — page 56

13. True — page 57

14. False — page 63

15. False — page 67

16. False — page 67

17. True — page 69

Remember, re-read any part you missed *before* you go on to the new learning on page 78. This is a very important aspect of good practice.

Active Participation by the Learner

Taking that test will do a great deal to increase your degree of learning and remembering, for you had to answer each question. It was not possible to passively sit and read without thinking. Your action demonstrates another important psychological generalization; *active participation by the learner increases his rate and degree of learning.* This active participation by the learner may be overt (observable by another person) or covert (not observable by another person). Writing the answers to our questions is overt because another person could observe your action. Thinking of the answers to our questions would be covert because another person could not tell whether or not you were doing it. The difference is the observable evidence produced by overt participation. No one but the learner can tell when he is participating covertly, his action must become overt before his teacher knows he has done it.

Both overt and covert responses are effective in increasing the speed and amount of learning. With younger learners we often require overt responses as this seems to help them focus on the learning task and gives us tangible evidence that they have. We ask them to "point," "raise their hands," "show me," etc. With more mature learners who have the mental discipline to maintain their focus, we often work with covert responses as we ask them to "think about," "consider these alternatives," "decide on which you prefer," and other similar stimuli for covert responding. A covert response is more efficient in terms of saving time. You can think of something faster than you can say it or write about it. An overt response is more efficient in terms of making sure your students are actively participating rather than day dreaming for it provides you with tangible evidence.

One of the problems with overt participation is that many teachers think it requires paper and pencil. This is not necessarily so; the response can be verbal or a signal such as raising hands, nodding heads, or forming the word with lips. In the case of a verbal response, usually only one person has an opportunity to make it. Teachers sometimes commit the error of saying, "John, what is the answer to question six?" The minute they hear the word "John," it is a signal to the other students that the participant (or pigeon!) has been chosen and their minds can remain at "idle" until the next question. To overcome this intellectual inertia, teachers need to ask the question of the whole group, *wait* so everyone can formulate a covert answer, and then call on someone for the audible response. That silence, with your eyes roving as you wait, is an excellent stimulus to thinking by your students. Even better is the identification of two or more plausible answers and then asking the whole class to show you by holding up fingers the number they would select if called on.

An example of this procedure would be writing on the board:

1. add
2. subtract
3. multiply
4. divide

Then, you would give verbal word problems asking all the students to hold up the number of fingers that would correspond with the number of the operation they would use to solve each problem. It's easy for the teacher to see which students know immediately, which need to take some time to figure it out, and which need to check with someone else's fingers before they know what to do. To eliminate the latter you can have them close their eyes and respond. With this technique, all students are overtly responding. It's not possible for them to put a studious look on their faces and then day dream. By such teaching you are stimulating active covert participation and then checking it with an overt response.

The trick is to get your students to actively participate in their learning either overtly or covertly so they don't just sit there while you wear yourself to a frazzle trying to teach them.

If you were working with a group of young learners, or older ones who were highly distractable, you would ask them to:

a. Say the answer in unison . . . . Turn to page 80, top
b. Think the answer . . . . Turn to page 80, bottom
c. Think the answer and respond with some signal so you could check the correctness of each . . . . Turn to page 81
d. Write the answer on paper . . . . Turn to page 82

a. You said you would ask them to say the answer in unison.

You're wise to know they need to respond overtly. However, with a group response it will be difficult for you to check who knows it and who doesn't. An enterprising lazy bone can make his mouth move and, unless you're a sophisticated lip reader, he'll get by with nothing but making noise. He may also verbally "hitch hike" as he hears the answer from others. Turn back to the question on page 79, and select an answer that will enable you to more nearly monitor each student's response so he feels accountable for coming up with a correct one.

b. You said you would ask them to think the answer.

Your effort to get a covert response out of each of them is laudable, but how are you going to know if you're successful? Some students have learned to turn on an intent look and turn off their mind. Use your good idea of making everyone think. Turn back to the questions on page 79, and, select an anwer that will let you know if you have been successful.

c. You said you would ask them to think the answer and respond with some signal so you could check the correctness of each.

You're a specialist in knowing how to get active participation from all your learners. You are asking them to respond covertly (thinking) which is efficient time-wise and will contribute to the habit of such responding. You also have the teaching know-how to hold them accountable by checking their answers. You may do this by some signal which will add vividness such as, "Touch your chin if you agree, touch your shoulder if you don't agree, and touch your elbow if you're not sure." Don't fall into the trap, "Raise your hand if you agree," because you don't know whether those not responding disagree or haven't made up their mind. Often it's a good technique to begin by asking those who haven't decided on the answer to use a signal. *Identify this group first and don't make it a sin to indicate they need more time or information before they decide.* Your overt response of selecting this answer indicates you don't need any more time or information on overt and covert active participation of the learner so turn to page 83.

d. You said you would ask each student to write the answer on paper.

You are wise to insist that everyone think (covert response) and then check by an overt response. The response you have chosen may give you trouble however. Thinking is faster than writing and presumably they all have the information necessary for thinking the selection of the right answer. We can be dead sure, however, they don't all have the same skills in translating that answer into writing. The time it takes will range from the short time necessary for an able writer to the eternity it takes to labor through the job by a "how-do-you-spell-it?" disability. And what do you do with the ones who are finished while you wait for the others?

If writing is an important part of the skill you're teaching, short written answers, with one person writing on the board for immediate knowledge of results, can be very effective. Whenever the whole class does something at once, you had better be sure they all have the skills available (information for selecting the right answer) and signal it. When there is a wide range of skills (ability to write that answer) you need to turn back to the question on page 79, and select an answer that can be more comfortably accomplished and you can move on.

Practice

We all have grown up with the platitude "Practice makes perfect." Don't you believe it! Again, knowledge of principles of learning makes the difference between efficient practice and practice which is a waste of time, yours and the learners.

We need to look at the question of how much practice is needed by a learner. The more the better? Not necessarily. Drill for drill's sake often can be a waste of time or actually deleterious to learning. Here again, results from research in learning can help us answer three important questions about practice: how much? how long? and how often?

In this book you have learned that there are many factors you can incorporate in a learning task which will eliminate the need for much practice. You will recall these factors are *motivation, sequence, meaning, vividness, degree of guidance, positive and negative transfer, and active participation by the learner.* Practice, however, is still a very important factor in how much we learn and how rapidly we learn. Appropriate practice is much more complicated than just "doing it over" or "doing it again and again." There are three important generalizations you must know and use if practice is to produce the learning results you seek. These generalizations will answer the questions:

1. How much of a learning task should you practice at one time?
2. How long (in time) should the practice period be?
3. How often should you have practice periods?

The answer to question 1 will tell us the best way to divide a learning task into parts. The answer to question 2 will help us know how many minutes to practice at one "sitting" and the answer to question 3 will help us decide whether we should practice several times a day, once a day, once a week, or once a month.

If we made an earlier part of this book meaningful, *that* learning should positively transfer, you will know the answer to the first question without any more practice. Let's see if you do. How much of a learning task should you practice at any one time?

a. A very small part.....................Turn to page 84, top
b. It all depends.....................Turn to page 84, bottom
c. The whole thing......................Turn to page 85, top
d. The smallest part that retains maximum meaning and does not waste the learner's time.............Turn to page 85, bottom

a. You said you would practice a very small part.

This would be a good idea if that small part had meaning, but would you practice a poem a word at a time or even a line at a time? We doubt it. Turn back to the question on page 83, and select an answer that reflects your good judgment in not trying to practice the whole thing at one time but also indicates you know how you should break up the task.

b. You said it all depends.

That it does, but on what? Turn back to the question on page 83, and select an answer that will tell you what generalization to depend on when you are trying to decide how much of a task to assign for practice at one time.

c. You said you would practice the whole thing.

In some cases you would be absolutely right. In other cases you would be doomed to failure. It would be folly to try to practice the whole play every time you rehearsed or the whole concerto every time you sat down at the piano. Turn back to the question on page 83, and select an answer that would tell you when you should practice the whole thing and when you should break it into parts.

d. You said you would practice the smallest part that retains maximum meaning and does not waste the learner's time.

You don't need any more practice on that generalization! You have learned it perfectly. As you learn (with meaning) smaller parts, you then can relate them to larger parts. For example, you might start with the plot of the whole play, so you maximize the meaning of the total. You begin your practice with just one scene, then the act that contains that scene, then other scenes and acts. Finally you put the whole thing together. It is important to remember, however, that you don't start practicing the episode until you know its relation to the total plot. Without this step you have not maximized the meaning of the episode. In the same way, when you are learning a piece of music or a poem, you begin with the whole thing to develop meaning and relationships but you start *practicing* the smallest part that is a unit such as 16 bars of music or the first stanza of the poem. Doing this will reduce the amount of practice necessary by increasing the amount of meaning and relationships. Hopefully, we have reduced the amount you need to practice, so turn to page 86.

Let's look at another example of how you would break up a learning task.

As a good teacher you have used meaningful word problems in mathematics that were related to the students lives (not pecks, bushels, rods, or "if you were a Canadian wheat farmer").

In solving these word problems it is necessary for students to be able to: 1) understand what the words say, 2) identify the question that is asked, 3) select the relevant facts that are given, 4) determine the mathematical operation to be used, and 5) compute the correct answer. Assuming that your students needed practice with all of these skills, how many of these skills would you work with at one time?

a. One skill.............................Turn to page 87, top
b. Two skills.........................Turn to page 87, bottom
c. All of the skills except computing
   the answer..........................Turn to page 88, top
d. All of them........................Turn to page 88, bottom

a. You said you work with one skill at a time.

Good for you because each one of them has meaning. Being able to read a problem and know what it's about is a necessary first step. (For a remedial reader, you may not hold him to this because it would delay unnecessarily mathematical skills he is capable of developing. You would read the problem for him and proceed to teach math.) Being able to determine the question asked is the next meaningful step before you can select the relevant facts or appropriate operation. Much of the students' inability to solve word problems is a result of being exposed to all of these sub skills at once so that they never really understand any. Also, if you do not work on each skill separately, you will never know which lack is causing all those wrong answers. You have the right answer so turn to page 89.

b. You said you would work on two skills at a time.

That might be a good idea if they were related, such as understanding the words and identifying the question. Usually, however, each skill is so important it needs to be stressed by itself. In this way, whatever skill the student doesn't possess can be learned before it's lack sinks the whole mathematical operation, discourages him, and persuades you he is unteachable. Turn back to the question on page 86, and select an answer that reflects the generalization "the smallest amount that is meaningful."

c. You said you would work with all of the skills except computing the answer.

You're wise to separate the "right-answer" fixation from the important understandings that are basic to its achievement. You have, however, cut out a herculean task for yourself by trying to practice so many important (and different!) skills at one time. Don't feel too badly if you have selected this answer. Thousands of teachers before you have done so. A nation of adults who feel they are mathematical incompetents has been the result. Turn back to the question on page 86, and select an answer that indicates you will "sin no more."

d. You said you would work on all of them.

Eventually you will need to but right now you are courting diaster, valiant though you be. Working on so many skills at once is not the wisest use of time. This is not to say that such behavior is more typical of classroom practice than the better answer you will surely choose when you turn back to the question on page 86.

Let's now turn to our second question. How long (in time) should the practice period be? How many minutes should a learner practice his multiplication facts? Spelling? A play? Speed reading to find answers? Running? Throwing a ball? Doing algebraic equations?

My goodness, you say, those are all different kinds of skills. There's no answer to that. You're right, there's no answer in minutes but there is an answer in terms of a generalization. Practice periods should be the *shortest amount of time in which it is possible to really work on the task.* A five or ten minute drill on multiplication or spelling will be ample time to get some learning accomplished. Three short practice periods a day will accomplish infinitely more than one long one. (That is assuming the students get to work and don't waste ten minutes getting started.) With other tasks, such as practicing a play, you will need a longer period to get something accomplished but two shorter practice sessions will usually accomplish more than one longer session. (Again this is providing there is not a lot of time wasted getting started.) As you learn each part of a task, your practice periods will become longer in order to get the job done of putting the parts together. (Practicing the whole act, the whole piece, etc.)

Understanding a new process in algebra, or reading complicated material, will take more time to accomplish. Therefore, we need to plan for a longer practice period. Ask yourself the question, "How much time will it take to really get something done?" and plan your practice periods accordingly. In most cases you are not trying to get it absolutely perfect the first time, this is one sure way to kill learning. Writing a spelling word 100 times or throwing a ball only one time are violations of this principle.

Suppose you want your students to develop more speed in their mathematical computation. How long would you make their practice periods:

a. About five minutes......................Turn to page 90, top
b. About fifteen minutes................Turn to page 90, bottom
c. About one half hour....................Turn to page 91, top
d. About one hour......................Turn to page 91, bottom

a. **You said you would have your students develop speed with practice periods that lasted about five minutes.**

You'll turn out world champions! Working at full speed for three to five minutes will give a great deal of practice in productive "hurrying." Trying to maintain that speed for long periods of time results in fatigue, which in turn results in practicing at slower speeds (which you don't want), to say nothing of the increase in mechanical errors. Of course as your students practice, they will be able to maintain their speed for longer periods, but remember, there's a difference in purpose between sprinters and distance runners. You know how to develop speed so turn to page 92, and decide what you would do with a different kind of assignment.

b. **You said you would have your students develop speed with practice periods that lasted fifteen minutes.**

That might be a good idea if your students already had developed considerable academic "muscle and stamina." Our guess is that they would need to take a more leisurely pace if they were to last 15 minutes. As a result, they would not be practicing at their maximum speed which is the behavior you want. To get the real "hurrying behavior" you were after, turn back to the question on page 89, and select a different answer.

c. **You said you would have your students develop speed with practice periods that lasted one half hour.**

Good luck! And you'll need it. Have you ever tried running as fast as you could for several blocks? You make a great beginning, but no one can last long at his maximum speed, so soon you begin to slow down and the majority of the time is a practice period for fast walking. If you wanted to practice only fast running, what distance would you select for yourself? Do the same thing for your learner as you turn back to the question on page 89, and select a different answer.

d. **You said you would have your students develop speed with practice periods that lasted one hour.**

While they are working, sit down and write the author of this book a letter explaining how this section should have been written so you didn't get such an outlandish idea. We know you are kidding so go back to the question on page 89, and *you hurry* to select an answer that will erase any possible negative transfer from this answer.

You have learned two important generalizations which will help you determine how much to practice and how long to practice at one time. You know you should select the *smallest amount of the task that has maximum meaning* for the learner and he should practice the *shortest time* that will permit him to feel he has really *accomplished* something.

Now, how often should we schedule these practice periods? Once an hour, once a day, once a week, or once a year? The latter suggestion sounds ridiculous, doesn't it? Look, however, at what happens in school. A subject is "covered" once in a year, be it the September spelling list or the Civil War and it is practiced no more. The results in June of such once-a-year teaching are only too apparent.

The generalization that guides us to speedy learning is *mass the practice at the beginning of learning.* This means make your practice periods frequent and closely spaced, usually more than once a day. If you wish your students to learn the multiplication facts, teach them (remember a *few* at a time) several times a day. You might schedule a five to ten minute "drill" period just before recess, another before noon and a third before afternoon dismissal. You'll be surprised at how fast they are learned. By scheduling them at the end of an instructional period, you'll avoid retroactive interference from subsequent learnings. (Remember the words at the end of the list were easy to learn.) If you dismiss each student who responds correctly, you will be rewarding the "saints" and giving the "sinners" the additional practice they need. Occasionally, you need to give a reluctant learner a combination you're sure he knows and let him be the first to leave. The "vividness" of his success in this experience will do wonders for his motivation to learn.

We hope you often divide your class into small groups for committee work and discussion. We also hope you free your students for individual study or projects. How long a time would you let students work at such assignments?

It depends on:

    a. The age of the students................Turn to page 93, top
    b. The purpose of the group..........Turn to page 93, bottom
    c. The subject area.....................Turn to page 94, top
    d. The skill of the students in working in
       such assignments................Turn to page 94, bottom

a. You said it depends on the age of the students.

Any age students contain all the ingredients for instant chaos. The only thing you need to add is the *wrong* amount of time even in a group under the direct supervision of the teacher. We have seen young children work successfully, individually, and in groups, for extended periods of time and we have seen high school students disintegrate in less than five minutes. How do you explain that? Of course older students can usually do most things for a longer period of time but turn back to the question on page 92, and select an answer that will guide you in independent work period.

b. You said it depends on the purpose of the group.

Of course it will take more time for them to design a program than to elect a chairman, but the former objective will take more periods not necessarily longer ones. The most important problem in small group work is to learn how to function as a member of one, and for some people that takes years. We don't think you believe we should schedule periods that long, so turn back to the question on page 92, and select an answer that will guide you in how many minutes you should schedule for each small group or independent work period.

c. You said it depends on the subject area.

If you found writing a play was harder for you than organizing a party, you would probably need longer periods in small groups to do that play. But what about the person who has just the opposite skills? A valid psychological generalization should apply to all learners. Turn back to the question on page 92, and select an answer that would help you determine the length of period for all learners.

d. You said it depends on the skill of the students in working in such assignments.

Your skill in applying learning generalizations is advanced! You're absolutely right. Students who have already developed the skills of being productive independently or in small groups can work longer regardless of the purpose, content, or age of students. (Of course younger students are less likely to have as much skill. They will have more, however, than older students who have never been taught the skill. If you doubt this, watch a PTA or a service club committee meeting.) Skilled students would resent a very short meeting because "getting something done" means really accomplishing something to them. To less skilled students "getting something done" might be merely selecting a subject or an area of work. You certainly "got that done" so turn now to page 95.

This principle of massing practice at the beginning of learning applies to all material, not just merely drill or rote memorization. If you want your group to rapidly learn some new concepts, introduce them (with examples to provide that essential meaning), review the essential ideas at the end of the period, come back to them again during the day, and review again just before going home. You have massed practice by providing four opportunities in one day. Don't think the learning is complete. The next day you will need to provide a couple of opportunities to deal with those same concepts, hopefully with some fresh examples. Again the following day you will need to work with them. You might skip the next day but be sure you return to those concepts on the fifth day. If that day is Friday, you will automatically skip the next two days but return to that learning for sure on Monday. You will probably need to practice only a couple of times this week and only once the following week. As material is well learned, you can leave longer and longer blocks of time between practice periods which is labeled as "distributing practice." *Massing practice at the initial stages of learning makes for fast learning. Distributing practice after material is learned makes for long remembering.* Knowing this psychological principle should help you resist the "once over lightly" temptation that sabotages much of our learning effort. If it's worth teaching at all, it's worth teaching so it is really learned and not forgotten tomorrow or next week. Do you recall how you crammed for some college exams and two days later remembered little or nothing of what you had "learned"? This is an example of the wastefulness of the "one shot" lengthy practice period. We hope you can also recall having courses that were so interesting you read and studied all through them. Much of that material you still remember, don't you? Meaningfulness and interest were factors in your retention but so was the fact that you distributed your practice.

The reason for scheduling massed practice at the beginning of learning is easily perceivable if you inspect learning and forgetting curves. You will find that the greatest "fall out" of forgetting occurs immediately after you stop practicing, and it is more extensive with material that is not well learned. Therefore, in the beginning stages of learning, the "fall" is considerable. You need to practice again quickly before learning goes back to the "zero" point. As material is better learned, it is not so susceptible to forgetting and an occasional practice period will keep it up to an acceptable point.

Without conscious knowledge of this principle most of us have trained ourselves to operate by it in our daily life. When we meet a person whose name we want to remember, we say it to ourselves many times sub-vocally. We need to review it several times until we can recall it readily and then an occasional practice keeps it in our mind. If on the other hand we meet a person, learn his name, and then don't see him for many months, most of us find our mind and memory blank. Repeating something over and over to ourselves (a phone number or set of directions) if we need to remember it, is another way we have learned to mass practice at the initial stages of learning.

When you introduce any new learning, be it a word, a behavior, a skill, an idea, a concept, names and dates, techniques, or what have you, good teaching implies you will practice or review it:

a. Several times the first day...............Turn to page 97, top
b. Several times the first week..........Turn to page 97, bottom
c. Several times the first month............Turn to page 98, top
d. Several times the first year...........Turn to page 98, bottom

a. You said you would go over it several times the first day.

You are absolutely right. You would be massing practice at the initial stage of learning. Also, hopefully, you are giving maximum guidance. That is what we have been trying to do as we asked several questions about practice. You have learned this principle and proved it by choosing this answer (active participation by the learner). We posed this question so you would "go over it again" before you went on to page 99.

b. You said you would go over it several times the first week.

You would certainly need to do that but you are taking a chance it won't be remembered the second morning, especially by the students who didn't really get it the first time. Turn back to the question on page 96, and select an answer that will make for more rapid and more sure learning.

c. You said you would go over it several times the first month.

That's an excellent idea provided it was well learned first. Otherwise, you will be wasting time by beginning with distributed practice. Turn back to the question on page 96, and select an answer that will ensure it is well learned quickly.

d. You said you would go over it several times the first year.

That's an excellent way to distribute your practice *after* something has been learned. Turn back to the question on page 96, and choose an answer that will *get* it learned quickly.

By now you should realize that the total time spent in practice is not nearly as important as the way that practice is scheduled. Suppose you could practice only one hour on some relatively simple learning. How would you schedule it?

a. Settle down for the hour and really
   learn it............................Turn to page 100, top
b. Learn it as well as possible in half-hour
   and then schedule another half-hour to
   review it at a later date.............Turn to page 100, bottom
c. Schedule four 15 minute periods
   in a week...........................Turn to page 101, top
d. Schedule three short periods the first day,
   two the second, one the third, skip the
   fourth, and use the time left for occasional
   reviews...........................Turn to page 101, bottom

a. You said you would settle down for an hour and really learn it.

Your determination is admirable but your practice theory isn't. If you didn't die of boredom or fatigue in that first hour you would probably have the material well learned. Your forgetting curve would match your learning curve however, and with no additional practice we doubt if your learning would endure. Remember the college cramming. Turn back to the question on page 99, and select an answer where your learning and remembering will match your determination.

b. You said you would learn it as well as possible in a half-hour and then schedule another half-hour to review it at a later date.

You are wise to schedule more than one practice period but you didn't carry the idea far enough. Our guess is that your learning would not prove resistant to forgetting after a period of time. turn back to the question on page 99, and select an answer that will take into account your knowledge of massed and distributed practice.

c. You said you would schedule four 15 minute periods in a week.

Your judgment is infinitely better than most teachers, but it does not reflect what you have learned about massing and distributing practice. You are not providing different schedules for initial and later stages of learning. Turn back to the question on page 99, and select an answer that will take this into account.

d. You said you would schedule three short periods the first day, two the second one, one the third, skip the fourth, and use the time left for occasional review.

You are an expert in practice theory and we don't have to worry about you in the classroom. Practice there what we have preached here and spread the "gospel" to other teachers.

You know from our response to your selection of this answer that you're doing very well in your learning. This knowledge of "how you're doing" is known as "knowledge of results" and is a very important factor in speeding up your learning. Turn to page 102, and learn how you can use *knowledge of results* to speed up your students' learning.

Knowledge of Results

When practice is merely "doing something over" or "again and again" it is not efficient and often not even productive. A person needs to know how he is doing, i.e., what he is doing correctly and therefore should continue, and what he is doing that needs to be changed or improved. The answer to the question "how am I doing" is known psychologically as *knowledge of results* and is essential for speedy and effective learning.

This principle is obvious if we think of a sharp shooter who took aim and shot, but never knew where his bullet went. He must have feedback of "a little too high," or "just to the left of the ten ring," if he is to improve his accuracy. Also obvious is the *more precise and specific the feedback, the more helpful it is* to him and the faster he will improve.

The necessity for precision and specificity of knowledge of results is just as important in any other type of learning. Students need to know what is right and wrong in their learning performance so they can continue the former and correct the latter. The principle was identified by Thorndike a half a century ago when he had students practice drawing what they estimated were four-inch lines. They drew hundreds of them and the last were no more accurate than the first. Then the students were asked to measure each line after they drew it so they would know to what degree it was too short or too long before they tried to draw the next one. In no time at all they improved tremendously because they had feedback which would help to direct them in each subsequent performance.

Reading this should cause you to do some introspection. How much knowledge of results is available to the learners for whom are responsible? Is it specific, such as "you did an excellent job in your introductory paragraph but your conclusion seeemd weak," or are you in the habit of a general "good work" or even worse, a grade? Yes, grades usually are *not* effective knowledge of results. An "A" can mean your work was excellent, the others were so bad yours looked great, the teacher felt charitable, you're the son of the superintendent, the teacher is an easy grader, need we go on?

102

In this book we have tried to give you specific knowledge of results as you selected the answers to questions. We told you why you were right and, if you were wrong, we suggested the thing you needed to consider in order to select the right answer. This should have increased your rate and degree of learning much more than if we had merely told you "right" or "wrong."

If you wished your students to learn to listen to each other in discussions, consider the idea they heard, and extend or refine those ideas rather than each student contributing an unrelated thought, you would use the principle of knowledge of results by:

a. Stressing the importance of listening to
   and extending ideas................... Turn to page 104, top

b. Signaling your approval to students
   who extended or refined ideas....... Turn to page 104, bottom

c. Tallying the number of times one student's
   ideas were extended by another........ Turn to page 105, top

d. Recognizing when a response indicated the
   person had really listened to previous
   speakers and pointing out how the idea
   had been extended or refined........ Turn to page 105, bottom

a. **You said you would stress the importance of listening to and extending ideas.**

We certainly hope you would do that in order to focus students on the reason for the behavior they are to practice. Now you need to do something to increase their speed in learning. Turn back to the questions on page 103, and select an answer that will increase their rate of learning while they practice this important skill.

b. **You said you would signal your approval to students who extended or refined ideas.**

You're on the right track, for students will know they are practicing the skill. This is in the category of saying "you're right," but for maximum gain in learning it needs to be more specific. Turn back to the question on page 103, and select an answer that will extend and refine *your* good idea.

c. You said you would tally the number of times one student's ideas were extended by another.

You are certainly giving quantitative knowledge of results, i.e., how many times the desirable behavior occurred. The qualitative dimension of how well it was done also needs to be incorporated to increase the speed with which students learn to make better and better responses. Turn back to the question on page 103, and select an answer that will extend and refine *your* good idea.

d. You said you would recognize when a response indicated the person had really listened to previous speakers and point out how the idea had been extended or refined.

By selecting this answer you are extending the generalization concerning knowledge of results into a precise and specific course of action. If you didn't select this answer in the first place, it was probably because you thought it would interfere too much with the discussion. You might be right, but remember that the objective of this particular lesson was to teach the skill of building on another person's idea, not to teach the skill of keeping the discussion going. If the latter had been our objective (and at times it should be), we would not be interrupting. By pointing out the specific behavior of listeners who extend ideas, each learner has a better idea of what he should practice and also knows when he has achieved it satisfactorily.

Obviously we can't have our students continue to practice everything they have learned for the rest of their lives, so turn to page 106 to find out when to stop practicing.

Overlearning

When is something learned to an extent that practice is no longer needed to maintain the skill? All of us have had the experience of remembering something that we haven't used or practiced for years. Being able to recite a poem learned in childhood, finding our way in a city after years of absence, and being able to conjugate a verb from a high school foreign language class are all examples which occur frequently. The opposite can also be true for sometimes we *cannot* remember how to perform these tasks. The difference between remembering or forgetting after a period of no practice can be due to several factors which are described in detail in a book in this series, *Retention Theory for Teachers*. Reading this book should result in your knowing about and being able to manipulate five important factors which will promote retention of whatever you teach.

You have already learned about distributing practice which makes for long retention, but it is also important for a teacher to know when something is so well learned that additional practice is a waste of time. We usually assume that when a task can be performed without errors it has been learned. This is true whether the task is the recall of a single name or date, the performance of a complex process in math, or the application of a concept or generalization to a completely new situation where it is appropriate.

As soon as we have evidence that any one of these tasks has been learned, that is, performed without error in distributed practice, should we stop practicing? Usually not, we should practice the now errorless skill of a few more times. The psychological terms for this additional practice when something has already been learned is *overlearning*. Overlearning accomplishes two important things. First, it eliminates the possibility that the correct response was merely a happy accident (getting the ball through the basket) or guess (selecting the correct answer from alternatives when you didn't really know). Second, it insures adequate practice of the correct response when often during learning there has been more practice of the wrong responses that lead up to the right one. Think how many times the ball has missed the basket or errors have been made in long division. Those efforts also have had practice, but of the wrong response. This is an important reason why we always try to have a learner achieve the correct response. Doing something wrong constitutes practice which will negatively transfer and interfere with learning the correct response.

Overlearning (practicing two or three more times after something has been learned) is efficient use of time. Practice after that can be a waste of time or even result in deteriorated learning performance. Look at any spelling word written one hundred times. The writing has gone to pot, the spelling may be incorrect, and we can guarantee that the learner's attitude is just the opposite of what one had hoped to achieve. It is much better to stop after a few correct responses and, after a period of time, check to be sure the performance is still correct. If it is, drop it for a longer period of time and check again. When your check reveals errors, practice again until you have two or three errorles performances and then move on to something new.

How well a student does on a learning or performance task often is related to how well he thinks he can do. Consequently, it is important that we consider his level of aspiration.

Level of Aspiration

The goal you estimate you can achieve is psychologically termed your *level of aspiration*. Its importance is related to the fact that an appropriate and realistic level of aspiration productively affects your rate and degree of learning. Suppose you were asked how long it would take you to put into practice everything you have learned in this book. If you said "Tomorrow morning," you might try hard but, unless you're an "infallible" teacher (and we've never seen one), you would be able to translate some of these learning principles into action but would bog down on others and forget a few. As a result of your unrealistic estimate of your ability to achieve this goal, you would probably decide the whole thing was too much for you, "abandon ship," and go back to your old ways of teaching.

Suppose in answer to our question you estimated, "It will take me at least ten years to incorporate these ideas into my daily teaching." We would predict that tomorrow morning (with ten years to go) you wouldn't be too concerned with changing your behavior and your teaching growth would proceed at a snail's pace.

Instead of these two unrealistic levels of aspiration, suppose you responded, "I'm going to take one principle of learning each week and really work on it until I incorporate it in my teaching behavior." Our guess is that the end result would be closely approximating that infallible teacher we've never seen before. Because you have a realistic awareness of the magnitude of the problem, knowledge of your ability, and realization of the two billion other things in teaching that demand your attention and sap your energy, you are setting an attainable goal. Because of your realistic level of aspiration, there's a good chance you will keep on working and achieve that goal.

Students operate in the same manner. Ask a disabled learner how much he can accomplish in the next period. Usually he'll set his objectives so ridiculously low he won't have to try or so unrealistically high the "brain trust" of the class couldn't achieve such a goal. As a result, in the first case he'll putter along or in the second case give up. In both cases he'll learn little or nothing.

If, instead of an inappropriate level of aspiration he sets an attainable goal, he'll probably work hard to achieve it and his learning will increase. The lesson for us as teachers is that we attempt to help students monitor objectively their own performances so they have a realistic notion of what they can achieve. Then, as with reasonable effort they achieve what they predicted, their motivation to learn will be increased. Their level of aspiration can be raised accordingly and their rate of learning will concurrently accelerate.

We are not suggesting you move in with hob nailed boots when a learner under-estimates of over-estimates his ability to perform but are urging you to help each student develop a realistic and thereby attainable level of aspiration so accomplishment of his goal becomes an important propellent to his future learning.

Overcoming a discouraged learner's inertia by suggesting he see if he can finsh the next question or problem in two minutes (or whatever time is appropriate) *and reinforcing him when he does*, sets a realistic goal and gives him a notion of an appropriate level of aspiration. The important principle here is related to: a) breaking the task into small meaningful parts, b) selecting a task that is possible for the learner to achieve, and c) *reinforcing* him when he does. We'll talk about this reinforcement in a few minutes but first let's check out your understanding of level of aspiration.

How could you use the factor of level of aspiration to increase reading speed? Would you:

a. Talk about readers who have achieved
   incredible speeds and encourage your learners
   to try to accomplish the same thing?.....Turn to page 110, top
b. Have each learner check his speed and
   work to become the fastest reader in
   the room?......................Turn to page 110, bottom
c. Have each learner check his speed and
   work to increase it by five or ten percent...Turn to page 111, top
d. Have each reader compare his speed
   with generally accepted speeds?.....Turn to page 111, bottom

a. You said you would talk about readers who have achieved incredible speeds and encourage your learners to try to accomplish the same thing.

It's amazing how commonly this kind of action occurs. Learners are often encouraged to be THE BEST whether it is in reading, high jumping, or president when they grow up. While such a level of aspiration may have temporary motivational value, the possibility of achievement of the goal often is so remote that in a short time the learner gives up and turns his attention to more attainable rewards like talking to his neighbor or doodling. We're glad you read this so you'll resist any temptation to dangle unrealistic goals in front of learners ("If you'd really try you could make straight A's" or the like.) Before you suggest a goal, be sure it's attainment is: 1) possible and 2) probable for this particular learner. Turn back to the question on page 109, and select the answer that has the ingredients of possibility and probability.

b. You said you would have each learner check his speed and work to become the fastest reader in the room.

You are wise to establish a base line from which each learner can work to improve his performance. Your wisdom needs to extend to the slowest student who has the greatest learning chore and the fastest student who has no chore at all. Both have inappropriate achievement goals. Turn back to the question on page 109, and select an answer which takes into account your good idea of base line of performance but also implies a realistic level of aspiration and an appropriate goal for each learner.

c. **You said you would have each learner check his speed and work to increase it by five or ten percent.**

You couldn't do a better job in applying your knowledge of level of aspirations. Each student has an attainable goal that is related to his present performance. As he achieves it, his motivation to achieve more will probably increase and his learning will proportionately accelerate. Your achievement of understanding of the role of level of aspiration in learning should encourage you to set for yourself the goal of applying that knowledge in your classroom. Now let's take a brief look at *reinforcement* on the next page.

d. **You said you would have each reader compare his speed with generally acceptable speeds.**

Your students' reactions would range from "I'll never make it" to "I've already accomplished it." Neither of these is conducive to productive effort. This answer would be appropriate only for the learner who was just enough below, that with some effort he could attain the acceptable speed and therefore that goal was an appropriate level of aspiration for him. Turn back to the question on page 109, and select an answer that would help all students set an appropriate level of aspiration for themselves.

Reinforcement

Reinforcement is a factor so important in increasing the rate and degree of learning that a whole book in this series has been devoted to it, *Reinforcement Theory for Teachers*. An understanding of this theory is probably the most useful tool a teacher can possess as he arranges an environment that will increase the students desirable learning and behavior as well as eliminate undesirable behavior. In fact, knowledge of reinforcement theory is usually the most important element in the elimination of discipline problems in the classroom.

The four important generalizations which will help you "shape" or "manage" your students' learning are:

1. Positive reinforcement will strengthen the behavior it immediately follows.
2. Negative reinforcement will suppress the behavior that brought it on and strengthen any behavior that takes it away. As a result, negative reinforcement can be dangerous. Better read *Reinforcement Theory for Teachers* before you use punishment in your classroom!
3. Extinction (no reinforcement whatsoever) eliminates most behavior.
4. Regular reinforcement (reinforcing behavior every time it occurs) makes for fast learning. Intermittent reinforcement (skipping sometimes) makes for long remembering. This is similar to massing practice for fast learning and distributing practice for long remembering.

We don't expect you to understand all this and be able to use it if you haven't read the book in this series which discusses these principles in detail and helps you put them to use in your classroom. We cannot recommend knowledge of reinforcement theory too strongly as an *essential ingredient* in your repertoire of teaching skills if you wish to increase the amount your students learn and the speed with which they learn it.

Throughout this book we have stressed some things you as a teacher can do and some of the things you can have your students do to make learning easier and more predictably successful. While the emphasis has been on your decisions for action we are well aware that how you and your students *feel* about what you and they are doing is an equally important factor in how much and how rapidly they learn. While feelings are much less tangible than action, they too are predictable in their effect on learning.

We usually categorize feelings of joy, excitement, pleasure, interest, success, and the like, as *pleasant feeling tones*. These act as propellents in learning situations so by all means encourage them in your classroom.

Feelings of unhappiness, frustration, anxiety, failure, and the like, are usually categorized as *unpleasant feeling tones*. Surprisingly, these too, act as propellents in learning but they can have undesirable side effects. Because of this contamination, proceed with caution if these feelings are present in any learning situation and consider whether or not you should work to eliminate them.

It may surprise you to realize that almost any feeling tones that are not excessive are an aid to learning. We would certainly hope these feelings would be pleasant. But other feeling tones, anxiety, suspense, discomfort, apprehension, pathos, also cause the learner to respond with greater vigor and involvement with the learning task. The result is often increased learning in less time (with hopefully no undesirable side effects).

Great works of literature, art, and music don't always produce pleasant feeling tones but make a powerful impact on feelings and, as a result, exert influence on learning. Pathos, tragedy, sorrow, and fear, as well as ecstasy, joy, and humor, contribute to meaning and vividness and consequently to the ability of the student to assimilate and remember a learning experience. We usually avoid the less desirable feeling tones because of their conditioning potential which may generate learnings we don't wish to occur. For example, fear may help to teach a subject but will also teach a learner to avoid it in the future. Tragedy may help to make a point but it may also result in depression that will interfere with future learning. The most important point for you to remember is not to allow the it-doesn't-make-any-difference climate of boredom and indifference to permeate your classroom. Instead, be aware of the learning propulsion from feeling tones and know that pleasant ones are most effective. Unpleasant feelings can contaminate the learning situation.

We would hope this book has left you with pleasant feeling tones. If there were any unpleasant ones, we trust they were due to a "why didn't someone teach me this before now?" feeling. The knowledge in this book is not new but previously it has existed only in psychological journals and was written in language that was not very meaningful to teachers.

To see how meaningful it now is to you, check your knowledge by answering the following questions on the last half of the book.

Mark the following true (T) or false (F)

_____1. Active participation by the learner means he does something the teacher can see.

_____2. Covert participation is more efficient in terms of time.

_____3. How much of a task you should practice depends on the length of the task.

_____4. In most cases many short practice periods are more effective than are long ones.

_____5. Practice should be massed at the initial stages of learning and then distributed.

_____6. The more specifically and precisely a student knows how well he is doing, the more he is apt to improve.

_____7. As soon as a student has a perfect response he can stop practicing.

_____8. Striving to be the very best is good motivation for learners.

_____9. The higher the level of aspiration the greater the learning.

_____10. A teacher's ability to use reinforcement theory is one of the most important factors in reducing or eliminating discipline problems.

_____11. Unpleasant feeling tones are a deterrent to learning.

_____12. You now are more sophisticated than most learning theorists in terms of application of the principles of learning to a classroom situation.

Turn the page and check your answers. Remember to re-read any part where you were not sure so you mass your practice for better learning.

1. False—page 78

2. True—page 78

3. False—page 83

4. True—page 89

5. True—page 95

6. True—page 102

7. False—page 106

8. False—page 108

9. False—page 108

10. True—page 112

11. False—page 113

12. True. *Yes you really are!* Good luck to you as you use them.